IN THE BLUE CORNER

In The Blue Corner
by Jerome Gage

ISBN: 978-0-615-87706-8

© 2014 Fight Log Media LLC.

All rights reserved, including the right to reproduce this book in whole or any portions thereof, in any form whatsoever.

For information regarding this book please contact:

        Fight Log Media LLC
        7739 E. Broadway Blvd #259
        Tucson, AZ 85710-3941

www.fightlogs.com

CHAPTER 1: WHO AM I?

"So I was wondering if you wanted to be in my corner this fight?" asked George. I looked at him, confused, thinking, *Is he serious? Who am I to be in someone's corner? I don't even fight.*

I grew up a Railroader's son and the youngest of four children, in the small Nebraska town of Maxwell, population: 230. Maxwell was located near North Platte, which is the home to the largest railroad yards in the world and a blue-collar area of the nation. It seems there are three types of people in the community: the first works on the railroad, the second works on a farm, and the third does both.

Most people chuckle when they hear the size of my hometown or when they discover my graduating class was comprised of nineteen people including me, but I thought it was extraordinary. Living in such a tiny town gives you the opportunity to, and are expected to, participate in everything, especially sports. From the age of six there are few times in my life when I wasn't competing in some fashion, but martial arts training opportunities were few and far between. At the age of ten, I experimented with Tae Kwon Do but I only lasted a year. Football was much more appealing to me. Despite always being the smallest person on the team I loved football, and occasionally, it loved me back.

After high school, I was awarded a modest football scholarship to a small private school called Concordia University. The friendly campus and the exceptional guys on the team made me feel right at home. I loved the atmosphere of the college game and the dedication everyone on the team had to the sport was inspiring. I didn't want to miss any of it. At the end of the season I was awarded the Ironman Award for never missing a practice. Unfortunately, after my freshman season I could see the writing on the wall; there wasn't much room for a 140-pound cornerback with average, at best, athleticism in college. Plus, the school was expensive and my scholarship was far from covering the full cost of tuition. I was forced to leave the school and transferred to the University of Nebraska at Kearney (UNK).

While studying at UNK, I became good friends with Division II All-American Wrestler, Justin Willuweit, or Willow as his friends called him. Willow regularly talked about wrestling. Wrestling was in his blood and he loved everything about it. At the time, I knew little about the sport. Although I grew up in Nebraska, where seemingly everyone wrestles, my high school didn't have a wrestling program. Instead, I joined the basketball team; however, at the towering height of 5'8", I wasn't much of a standout. Listening to Willow speak about wrestling, I instantly became interested in the sport. I attended nearly all of the UNK home meets and began learning the names of the moves, positions, and famous wrestlers. Prior to befriending Willow, I never heard of Dan Gable, who is one of the most legendary wrestlers of all time; suddenly I had become a huge fan of the sport and wanted to learn more. Kearney was a small town of 30,000 people and in the late 1990's, the community offered little prospect to learn how to wrestle or do any sort of grappling. My experience never went beyond spectating back then, but I admired the sport nonetheless.

After college, I was offered a law enforcement position in Tucson, Arizona. Growing up in Nebraska, I knew little about Tucson or the entire state of Arizona for that matter. In college I took a spring break trip to Lake Havasu City, but that was a long way from Tucson, and that trip was mostly a blur anyway. I waited twenty-two months from the time I applied before the job became available. Luckily, at that stage in my life I was mobile. When the job offer came on a Thursday afternoon they informed me that if I accepted, I needed to be in Tucson by Sunday evening.

Excitedly, I jumped at the chance and immediately ran into my boss's office and resigned. Although I was ecstatic, my only predicament was that I was penniless. I was working in a call center for a sporting goods company called Cabela's and volunteered my spare time to coach Maxwell's high school football team. I had no money in the bank and refrained from asking my parents for financial help. I was yearning to become independent and I wanted to be responsible for myself. I took out a thousand dollar loan from the Union Pacific Credit Union (with my dad co-signing), just so I could afford the plane ticket. In the fall of 2003, I left my family and friends in Nebraska and flew to Arizona, a place where I knew no one.

Not long after finishing the academy I joined a softball team to stay competitive. I loved baseball growing up, but soon found out that softball just wasn't for me. I was also frustrated with the lack of consistency from other players on the team. Many times I drove across town during rush hour traffic only to determine that not enough players on my team had shown up, causing us to forfeit the game.

I needed a different sport. One night in late 2004, I saw a kickboxing match on ESPN. A fighter by the name of Cung Le was dominating his sport. The announcers were calling his style Sanshou. I began searching the internet to scout out a gym to train in it. Unfortunately, Sanshou wasn't a popular martial art and nowhere in Tucson offered it. However, during my search I did find a few Muay Thai gyms. Muay Thai is a kickboxing style originating from Thailand. It focuses on striking with the fists, elbows, knees, and shins. It also has a great emphasis placed on the *clinch*, which is a term for controlling your opponent with your hands on the back of their head making it difficult for your opponent to move and strike efficiently. Another reason I liked the idea of Muay Thai was the lack of the traditional martial arts gi (the uniform worn in Japanese and Korean martial arts) and katas (forms), which I was exposed to in my younger years in Tae Kwon Do. The uniform in Muay Thai consisted only of shorts, t-shirt, and gloves.

It wasn't Sanshou, which is what I was searching for, but everything I read online had high praise for Muay Thai so I jumped in with both feet and signed up at a popular gym in town. My instructor was only twenty-one years old but impressive. Never had I seen such powerful kicks from an individual. This made me eager to learn more. It worked out perfectly that the gym was only a few miles away from my house. I would run to the gym in the evenings for class then run back home.

Prior to our Muay Thai class, a Brazilian Jiu Jitsu class used the mats. I knew of jiu jitsu from the Ultimate Fighting Championship (UFC) videos I watched in the past and marveled at videos of Royce Gracie beating much bigger fighters in a cage. I also took a casual interest in the UFC during college after watching a young man named Tito Ortiz on the Fox Sports Network's show *The Best Damn Sports Show Period* tell the audience he would destroy Mike Tyson in a cage fight—an absolutely outrageous statement when Tyson was still feared in the sport.

Oftentimes, when I arrived to the gym early I would watch the jiu jitsu class closely. The class intrigued me, but I had no real interest in learning any of it. Mainly, I did not want to dress up in the dorky gi I hated as a kid again and roll on the ground with another guy. I merely wanted to learn how to knock people out.

I was able to keep up this routine of Muay Thai throughout the summer of 2005. Then life happened. The new chief at work decided to change our work shifts. Working the early morning shift the whole summer allowed me to train at night, but the new rules changed that. I was required to rotate shifts every three months. This meant that based on the Muay Thai schedule at the gym, I would only be able to train three months out of the year. Since I had been training hard and improving significantly, this made me very upset.

One night I was complaining to a friend at work that I was no longer going to be able to train. A guy named Kevin Jones (KJ), who just moved to Tucson from San Diego, overheard our conversation. KJ heard my complaints and asked, "Have you ever thought about training any Brazilian Jiu Jitsu? I have some mats in my garage and I've been thinking about teaching classes out of there. I'm having my first class this Saturday if you want to stop by."

Admittedly, I had my reservations. Despite being a huge fan of wrestling and watching many hours of jiu jitsu before my Muay Thai class I didn't have a burning desire to learn. However, I needed to do something and as I was being forced to give up Muay Thai, I gave it a shot.

KJ was a purple belt under Roy Harris, who was one of the first twelve non-Brazilians to receive his black belt in Brazilian Jiu Jitsu. He was running classes a couple times a week out of his garage. The very first day KJ opened up his garage I was there. My reservations turned out to be completely unfounded—I was hooked. I watched KJ roll with guys in class with seemingly effortless movements. He flowed as he went against men who were much larger than him and he made it look simple. To a smaller guy like me, who gave up football mainly because of my size, this was extremely appealing. Since that day it has been my goal to know as much as humanly possible about jiu jitsu.

At first, an arrangement was made to pay KJ one hundred dollars for him to teach me jiu jitsu. Then, as the classes increased in size and we needed more mat space, I pitched in for additional mats. However, one hundred dollars was all I ever paid him. The classes got bigger, as did the mat space, but he would never accept my money. Many nights the class would just be KJ and me, and I would get a free two-hour private lesson. Mark, who was a purple belt, was also a consistent member of the group. The two of them would spend hours submitting me with what seemed like mystical powers, but I kept returning. These two men dumped an obscene amount of time and knowledge into me.

The garage saw plenty of members over the years. It was like any other jiu jitsu gym: some competed, some fought, some were solid for six months then never came back. At one point we created a logo and called ourselves Saguaro Jiu Jitsu when we competed in tournaments in Las Vegas. The garage was the best thing that ever happened to me personally; for a paltry one hundred dollars I was given the gift of jiu jitsu and life-long friends.

I first met George Roop in the summer of 2007 at a small jiu jitsu tournament in Phoenix called Desert Quest. This tournament was a gi and no-gi competition that took place on a monthly or bimonthly basis. Normally jiu jitsu tournaments are separated into various divisions based on age and experience. The gi division is often based on the color of the belt. Brazilian Jiu Jitsu has five main adult belts that a practitioner will progress through: white, blue, purple, brown and black. In no-gi brackets the competitors are normally separated by years of experience. Desert Quest tournaments had no age brackets and no separation between experience or belts. A brand new white belt in his first tournament here could compete against a purple or brown belt.

Mark knew George previously from training at another gym. George's tall lanky body type does little to lead you to believe he is a professional athlete competing in one of the most elite fighting organizations in the world. He stood about 6'1" and at the time of our meeting weighed less than 160 pounds. George and I were in the same no-gi bracket and Mark introduced us before our matches.

Sadly, I lost in the second round of the tournament. I absolutely despise losing. It has always been embarrassing for me and this time was no different. In the second round, I fought against a kid who just turned eighteen and was entering the adult competition bracket. After he won on points, I thought to myself, *How humiliating to be defeated by a young punk kid.* I soon learned that was the way it goes sometimes – jiu jitsu is one of the rare sports where expertise often matters more than size or strength.

As I was changing clothes in the locker room of the Mesa Recreational Center, George walked in. He was putting on his gi for the gi division of the competition. I had little exposure to the gi let alone compete with it on. I felt intimidated by gi competition. I trained for less than two years and a majority of it was in no-gi. I was worried about being embarrassed if I competed in those matches because I wasn't familiar with the principles of the gi. In my opinion, the gi was wrestling with training wheels (or in my case a straight jacket) and that took away the fun of the sport. I preferred the lack of restriction of no-gi competition, in which competitors wore a tight synthetic shirt called a rash guard and board shorts. It was just you and the other guy; there was no heavy canvas gi to grasp. With a gi, it's easier to keep ahold of your opponent, and many chokes use the collar of the gi to force the other guy to submit or be choked into unconsciousness. Gi and no-gi competition is about 80% the same, but it's the other 20% that can get you in real trouble if you have not trained with it on.

While in the locker room, George asked if I would be interested in meeting from time to time to train. He went on to tell me that he fought in MMA and had difficulty finding training partners our size. Now, based on my first impression, George wasn't someone I normally envisioned hanging out with on a regular basis. When George spoke, he abused the language with words like "dude", "bro" and "dawg". Having grown up in Nebraska, I was raised with a fairly conservative attitude. Combine my upbringing with my career choice, and the "dude" and "bro" crowds didn't seem to be my kind of people. Over the years of knowing George, I began to appreciate this about him. It showed a sign of genuineness that had become a rarity in my life. In a world where most everyone is trying to impress someone or brownnose his or her boss, someone who speaks without pretense is refreshing. Despite my initial hesitation, George appeared to be a good guy, and I agreed to train and help him prepare for fights when needed. We exchanged phone numbers and I told him to contact me whenever he wanted to train.

Soon after, George called and asked me to train at his gym with him and a friend. When I arrived, George introduced me to Ed West. Ed was a smaller guy, about 5'7" and 150 pounds. He was the champion of Rage in the Cage, a smaller mixed martial arts promotion, and I was interested to see if I could keep up with him on the mats and in the ring. I quickly established that Ed was way out of my league and one of the best athletes I had ever come in contact with.

I trained with Ed and George once a week for a while. They would also join me at KJ's garage to practice. KJ lived on the outskirts of Tucson in a small community called Vail. In the world of jiu jitsu, people often have less respect for you if you don't train at a traditional school. Consequently, when I mentioned to people I trained in a garage in Vail, Arizona, some didn't take me seriously. Even so, the people who had the opportunity to train in KJ's garage knew that it was hard work and there was plenty to learn.

The jiu jitsu community in Tucson was very segregated. Cross-training (training at another school) was often not allowed. Many athletes who were members of the traditional BJJ schools in Tucson were prohibited to train at another school, and if they attempted, they were generally not welcomed. The garage was different. We enjoyed having people grapple with us from the different schools around Tucson, and most of the instructors of these schools permitted their students to train with us. We posed no threat to anyone's business and the garage was more of a club versus a school. This type of open-minded training environment was tremendously beneficial to all of us who had the chance to be a part of it.

I continued to roll with George and Ed when time allowed, but because of my work schedule I wasn't able to join in very often. I was working extremely long hours on constantly varying shifts. The extended hours of work combined with the long hours of training were difficult to keep up with. George and Ed continued to train and fight, chasing their dreams.

In March of 2008, George said he was going to Boston to try out for the Ultimate Fighting Championship's reality show *The Ultimate Fighter*. As we continued our talk, he informed me he had a fight in Denver the same weekend as the tryouts. I had my doubts about him making the show for a couple reasons. George was physically tough as nails and mentally stronger than most, but I was concerned about his level of experience. I had no vast amount of experience in training, but I speculated he might be considerably greener than other fighters at the tryouts. Higher profile fighters even auditioned for previous seasons and had not made the cut. Secondly, not fighting out of a high profile gym like Extreme Couture, Team Quest, or American Top Team would not favor George. Fighting out of a small gym in Tucson was not going to open any doors on its own, and going to the tryouts the day before a fight was going to put him at a disadvantage against others who only had one commitment that week.

George flew to Boston for the audition then immediately flew to Denver for his fight, which he won with a first round knockout. George made it to the final cut and eventually was offered a spot on the show. After getting to know him and seeing him fight on a national stage, I was very proud of him. George was given the chance to live the American dream by making his goals of fighting professionally a reality.

That season of *The Ultimate Fighter* ended and afterwards George stayed in Las Vegas and trained in more distinguished gyms. We stayed in touch and I went to Las Vegas to watch him fight in UFC 98, his first fight after the reality show's finale. Watching one of my training partners fight in front of thousands of people felt like a success for me. I was honored to have helped play a role—however small—in that accomplishment. I was certain I would have nothing more to offer him as a training partner because he had access to work with much more talented and knowledgeable martial artists.

As George followed his ambitions, I maintained my concentration on jiu jitsu and grappling. I had no real inclination to ever compete in MMA; the idea of being punched in the face in a cage didn't appeal to me. Yet, I was hooked on jiu jitsu. My work situation improved as well as I was selected to join an investigations team, providing me the much-needed flexibility for my training schedule.

An ancillary benefit to this new position was that it required schooling in a whole new set of enforcement skills. As such, I traveled on a frequent basis for training. I developed a sort of "have gi, will travel" mentality. Whenever work sent me out of town, the first thing I did was look up the closest MMA or BJJ school and dropped in. Having this type of mindset and opportunity gave me extensive exposure to many different styles and levels of jiu jitsu. I trained with guys such as Louie Cercedez, who fought in underground fights before MMA was sanctioned, Brazilian Jiu Jitsu World Champion Bernardo Faria, jiu jitsu legend Sergio Penha, members of the Royal Canadian Mounted Police, Division I Wrestlers, black belts, brown belts, pro fighters, and a Navy SEAL. If someone wanted to train, I did too. I was given the resources to meet amazing and talented people in gyms all across the country and learn from them.

George continued to fight in the UFC until he was released after losing two out of three fights. He then did one local fight and was picked up by World Extreme Cagefighting (WEC). At the time, WEC was the best place in the world for lighter fighters. Mixed Martial Arts has many different promotions. The top promotion in the world is the UFC. The UFC's lightest weight bracket at the time was lightweight at 155 pounds. The elite top-level fighters who were too small for the lightweight division often found themselves in the slightly lower-tiered promotion, the WEC, which was owned by the same parent company as the UFC, Zuffa, LLC. When George fought in the UFC, he was in the lightweight division. But George normally weighed around 160 pounds, so he often fought much larger fighters. Many fighters have mastered the art of cutting weight. It is not uncommon for fighters to cut from 180 pounds to 155 for weigh-ins. Fighters then have twenty-four hours to put much of that weight back on. This meant George could be outweighed by as much as twenty pounds on fight night. The WEC was a much better organization for George because they had lighter weight divisions. This allowed him to fight at his natural weight class of 145 pounds (featherweight) and he even fought once at 135 pounds (bantamweight). After the UFC absorbed the WEC in 2010, George found himself fighting in the UFC once again, only this time at 145 pounds.

George returned to Tucson, which brought him back together with his long time training partner, Ed, who had been fighting in the Bellator tournaments. Once the WEC was absorbed in to the UFC, there was room in the market for a new MMA organization thus bringing Bellator into the limelight. Bellator had a roster of tough fighters and a different idea. They made their fights a tournament-style match up to declare their champions. An MMA tournament is similar to one in soccer or the playoffs of other sports: you fight, and if you win, you move on to your next opponent. This continues until the two best fighters face off in the cage. Bellator was also promoting lighter weight classes, and Ed was a perfect fit in their organization.

In the fall of 2011, George signed on to go against a Japanese fighter by the name of Hatsu Hioki. Hioki was a dangerous fighter who was ranked number two in the world by various ranking systems. Hioki fought in Japan but had impressive wins over many distinguished fighters including Mark Hominick, who defeated George a year prior. George just finished an impressive win over a young tough fighter named Josh Grispi and there was a lot of excitement about this matchup with Hioki.

George has a reputation for not turning down fights. His decision to accept the Hominick fight in early 2011 surprised me since Hominick was his training partner in Las Vegas. This reputation to fight anyone, anywhere has given George the chance to derail some rising stars' plans, like his knockout victory over Jung Chan Sung, "The Korean Zombie". At times, the organizations will feed certain fighters match-ups that are favorable to them. By doing this the organization can increase the popularity of the fighter which in turn leads to more publicity for future fights. George, on the other hand, has served as the gatekeeper to the upper echelon of the UFC in the featherweight division. He has taken the fights against the organizations' rising stars on more than one occasion. He usually accepts the fight, and matchmakers always appreciate a fighter who is willing to take a fight, no matter who the opponent. The Hioki fight was one of these.

For the Hioki fight, one of our mutual friends contacted several jiu jitsu guys from town and asked us to help George gear up for the match. When I was called, my life was settling down. I had not competed in over a year. I was dating an amazing girl, Bernice, who lived in Phoenix, so a majority of my weekend time was spent either traveling to Phoenix or hanging out with her when she visited me in Tucson. I was still training and teaching a no-gi grappling class in my spare time while still working as an investigator. I earned my purple belt from KJ and Roy Harris earlier that year, which was a big personal accomplishment for me.

When I began training, KJ was a purple belt. The knowledge and expertise he possessed then was a major reason I wanted to learn more. Earning my purple belt and coming to terms with the idea that I was approaching the level KJ had been when I started was a proud moment for me. Being asked to help George prepare for the Hioki fight was another intensely gratifying moment and I jumped at the occasion to be a part of the training.

It was no secret Hioki had very impressive jiu jitsu, including some devastating triangles, a style of choke performed by squeezing your opponent's head and arm between your legs. Normally this choke is applied from a bottom position, but Hioki was able to secure this choke from side control and mount (top positions on the ground) in many fights. A mutual training partner, Brandon, and I studied many of Hioki's fights to discern his setups for these triangles and the control methods he used. In preparation for the

Hioki fight, George and I trained a couple times a week. I spent many rounds in side control and mount and we worked on George's defense from these positions. Going into the fight, we believed George would have the advantage in striking; therefore, we spent numerous hours working on defense for Hioki's strongest positions.

The Hioki fight proved us right. Despite losing a controversial decision, George performed superbly. The first round was extremely close, and as I watched the fight on television, I observed George's stand up striking was vastly superior to Hioki's. In my opinion, that alone should have been sufficient to win George the first round. The second round Hioki scored a takedown and George found himself on his back for the majority of the round. I watched this with immense nervousness. This situation alone would allow George to either reap the benefits of our hard work in practicing specifically for this situation or show that I had no idea what I was talking about. Of course I wanted George to win, but I surely didn't want our plan for defending the positions to be the reason he lost.

George executed perfectly. For every control and offensive move Hioki attempted, both in side control and mount, George had the answer. It was just as we rehearsed time and time again. Despite George's delay in escaping, it was obvious that Hioki's inability to finish the fight from his favorite positions frustrated him. In the third round, George continually placed Hioki on his back and rained down strikes. After round three, there was no doubt in my mind: George won that fight.

When the hand of Hioki was raised on a split decision, my heart sank. I assumed George would be crushed. He performed well and fought his heart out but still came up short. I failed in showing him ways to escape faster. The preparation to thwart the efforts of Hioki's offense left George at a disadvantage and we should have focused on escaping the position more than defending the offense. I believed if we worked on the same problem differently it could have helped him more.

The next day George called. Surprisingly, he wasn't as disappointed as I thought he would be. He said, "Hey bro, I just wanted to tell you thank you. He didn't have anything for me when he was in side control. I knew what he was doing the whole time." I responded by saying he did well and I was proud of him, and we hung up. Still, I felt I let him down.

CHAPTER 2: FIGHT PLAN

A month later, George asked me, "So I was wondering if you wanted to be in my corner this next fight?" My first instinct was to blurt out, "Well, hell yes I do!" Yet, I wondered if I had the knowledge and discipline it would take to help him win his fight. Could I be in his corner in the heat of a fight and give him the advice he needed? The only real cornering experience I had was helping a buddy in a "Battle of the Badges" interdepartmental police boxing event and coaching people for jiu jitsu and grappling tournaments. But this was more serious, with money, reputations, and careers on the line.

This fight was viewed as a must-win for George. Although he was now a seasoned veteran in the UFC, he had yet to put together two wins in a row. In a fast-growing sport like mixed martial arts, there was no shortage of younger fighters with fresher faces that the UFC would love to sign. If George lost this fight after dropping his last one to Hioki, it wouldn't take a stretch of the imagination to see he was edging closer to the chopping block in the UFC.

Before I answered him, I thought hard. If I was going to do it, it was vital to give George everything I could in the most professional manner. The fight had serious career implications for him, and I needed to bring my A-game. Finally, I responded, "Absolutely, I'd be honored to be in your corner."

That night, George revealed something that gave me the biggest boost of confidence of my life. He said, "Look, I'm not asking you to do you a favor. I'm asking because I believe you're a guy that can help me win this fight." These words were profound. I had never seen myself in this light. In my mind there were dozens of more qualified people in Tucson to be his corner, and six of them were on the mats with us at that moment. I had no in-depth knowledge of fighting. I was just a thirty-two-year-old purple belt with mediocre athleticism and sub-par striking skills. How did he think I could help him win this fight? No answer came. Although it felt reassuring to hear those words, I wasn't sure I could back those words up. Not wanting to let George down, I was going to do everything humanly possible to prepare him for the fight.

Once I arrived home that evening, I purchased my plane tickets. I thought it was odd that the biggest Mixed Martial Arts promotion in the world didn't even pay for their fighter's trainers. It turns out that each fighter receives two plane tickets, one for the fighter and one for a cornerman, and one hotel room for everyone to share. The remainder is on the fighter to supply. George was scheduled on the UFC on the Fox 2 card in Chicago. The fight was set for January 28, 2012. Only six weeks remained before his match. The other two cornermen were George's long-time training partner Ed and another man named Pierre.

A few days later, I arrived to George's house to watch tape. George was scheduled to fight against Cub Swanson. Cub was without a doubt a talented opponent. I watched him fight many times before, but never for the purpose of devising a plan to beat him. George and I watched six of Cub's fights. After dissecting them we noticed a few key points:

1.) Cub advances on the other fighter with his head down.

2.) In earlier fights, he was well disciplined with his hand position, but now he holds his hands fairly low.

3.) While on his back and in the guard, he continually uses a combination of a wrestler's switch, guillotine, and kimura to his right side only.

4.) Cub had a great habit of punching off every break or separation of the fighters.

5.) His favorite takedown was a hip toss.

6.) Cub threw very wide, looping punches and did not utilize his jab often.

Based on our observations, George's game plan was to work on taking advantage of the holes in Cub's game, such as:

1.) Throwing straight punches and utilizing many jabs.

2.) When Cub advanced toward his opponent, throwing wide punches with his head down, George would knee Cub's ducked head.

3.) Work on taking the back when he used the switch from the guard.

4.) Work on guillotine defenses.

5.) George needed to cover up on every break.

While preparing, George trained mainly at his home gym, which was across town. At times, he brought some of his training sessions to Boxing Inc., the gym at which I taught. Zac, the owner of Boxing Inc., was more than happy to have him in the gym. Many of the gym's instructors have boxing backgrounds and they have a solid group of amateur and professional boxers.

KJ and I taught no-gi grappling classes at Boxing Inc. and we started to see an influx of people joining the grappling program. We had a respectable core of training partners for George: KJ (now a black belt), Chris Cariaso (a UFC flyweight fighter), Brandon Roberts, (who had been George's very first MMA coach), and Jay Petersen. Boxing Inc. was the perfect gym for George's training. The environment of the gym and team-like atmosphere allowed

George to get the attention he needed to prepare for the fight.

Before Christmas, we had some great training. Days began with a light warm-up of flow grappling, when two people wrestle with very little resistance. This style of grappling allows the athlete to warm up muscles while working on transitions from position to position. Then George would work on a skill. Cub provided a unique set of challenges. The fight footage showed when Cub was taken down, he would promptly sit up in the guard, throw his left arm over the shoulder of his opponent's left shoulder and grab the inside of his opponent's left thigh. This is similar to a switch often used in wrestling. Generally our session of training consisted of transitioning out of this position, stepping over Cub's leg and taking his back.

After the skill session it was time to put in the fun work. A fighter needs to enter a match in tiptop condition. It is amazing how many fighters at the professional level begin a fight then be completely out of gas by the second round. I have often wondered if this happens because a fighter lacks a type of cardio training before a fight. Many fighters use strength and conditioning coaches to make sure they are in prime shape. George is no different. I think conditioning is very specific. As a high school athlete, I moved from football to basketball, however, after the first week of practice it was easy to see that "football shape" was not the same as "basketball shape".

Fighting is the same way. During grappling sessions we used the shark tank method to make sure George was in shape. We ran him through 8-12 five-minute rounds of grappling. Halfway through each round a fresh guy would replace his opponent. This type of training is physically and mentally exhausting, but worth it when it comes time to fight.

The holidays were fast approaching and I was going to Nebraska for Christmas. I felt like I was abandoning George, but I knew he had plenty of high-quality training partners and his training wouldn't miss a beat while I was gone.

CHAPTER 3: NEBRASKA

I was excited to go home for Christmas. There was no place to train but the seldom week away from the mat is a good thing. For me, a couple weeks away from the desert is refreshing. To an outsider, the town I grew up in may not be ideal, but to me it will always be home. My eldest sister Pam lives in North Platte, which is normally where I stay. North Platte's blue-collar roots appear in every area of the city. The conversations are dominated by stories of co-workers on the railroad, hunting excursions, or high school stories of the past. The town has a tough style that rivals any of the so-called "cowboy towns" of the Southwest.

Despite only being a town of 24,000 people and being in the middle of nowhere, North Platte has produced some tough athletes who have become local heroes. Two of them have made their mark on the fighting scene. Luke Caudillo, who made a couple appearances in the UFC, had long been the pride of the North Platte fighting scene before he left to train in Colorado. Another who made a big impact is Ryan Shultz. Shultz won the lightweight title for a former high-profile fight league called the International Fighting League (IFL). He achieved the title in an impressive fashion on Fox Sports Network, just prior to the IFL going out of business. The true hero of the town just became prevalent in the last few years. A young man named Danny Woodhead was now making his mark in the National Football League for the San Diego Chargers and before that, the New England Patriots.

Traveling home is never an easy feat. One of the disadvantages of growing up in a rural area is the lack of a direct airport to fly into. Maxwell lies along Interstate 80, halfway between Omaha and Denver. Visiting home means flying into Denver, renting a car or having someone pick me up, then driving another three to four hours to Maxwell. With the unpredictable weather and extremely cold winters of Nebraska, this can become cumbersome. I have made the drive from Denver to Maxwell at thirty-five miles per hour in the past due to the ice on the roads.

On December 16th, I flew into Denver and spent the next couple days visiting my best friend. Then I headed to Nebraska in time to watch my nephew, Dylan, wrestle. Dylan was a junior in the same high school I attended. Maxwell High School finally had a wrestling program, and Dylan was becoming a solid wrestler. I enjoy flying home once a year to catch one of his meets. Wrestling in the Midwest is just as popular as basketball, if not more so. Many wrestlers in Nebraska start as young as five years old. Dylan didn't begin the sport until he was in eighth grade, but he developed quickly and was building a good reputation as a wrestler.

However, that year's Christmas trip wasn't memorable because of time spent with friends, sports, or even good times. The trip that year would be a stark reminder of how fragile our lives really are.

I grew up on a small rectangular-shaped twenty-acre piece of land five miles south of Maxwell. Even though we didn't live on a farm, we definitely lived in the country. My dad purchased the land from his grandfather in the early 1970's and built a house on the north side of the property shortly thereafter. On the south side of the land, there once stood a trailer house where my paternal grandmother, Violet, and my step grandfather, Delmar, lived. My biological grandfather, Leroy, passed away when I was young. He was diagnosed with Parkinson's disease and my grandma spent many years taking care of him.

Years after Leroy's passing, my grandma placed a "Meet a Mate" ad in the local paper, simply asking for a "non-smoker, non-drinker who didn't use drugs and liked sports". Delmar fit the bill perfectly.

On April 3, 1988, my grandma married Delmar Bissell, and they moved into the house on the south end of our property. Delmar was a soft-spoken, God-fearing man. He wasn't my biological grandpa, but he was as close to any real grandpa I had on my dad's side of the family. Delmar was a gentleman, always putting my grandma first.

The hardest part of moving away from home has always been visiting home. When you can only visit once or twice a year, you witness the progression of aging in a much more noticeable fashion.

The Christmas of 2008, I noticed Delmar was no longer himself. He was becoming easily confused in daily casual conversations. The night we celebrated our family Christmas, he spent most of the night outside.

"Jerome, come out here and look at this, would ya?" Delmar said, coming into the house briefly. "I can't figure out how to shut this light off in the pickup. It will run down my battery."

I followed Delmar outside.

"See that blinking light?" Delmar said, pointing to the blinking blue light of his car alarm. "How do I get that off?"

"Well, it doesn't shut off, Delmar. That's your car alarm light. It blinks so people will know you have an alarm so they don't try to steal your truck," I said. I was surprised he would ask such a question, since he owned the pickup for a couple years.

"What? You think someone is going to steal my truck?"

"No, that's just why the light is here. There isn't anyone that is going to steal your truck."

"It's going to run down my battery."

"No it won't, Delmar. A lot of trucks have that. My truck has the same thing. You can't shut it off."

"Jerome, I need to get this to shut off. I can't afford to replace a battery."

The conversation continued in the same pattern the whole night. I couldn't convince him to leave the light alone. The next morning he never mentioned a thing about the light, as if it had never happened. I noticed then that he was starting to miss a step, but what I didn't know was that night would be the last time he ever called me by name.

The following years, Delmar's health faded fast. My grandma found herself having to care of her husband again. This time it didn't take long before she realized it was just too much at her age. They moved into an assisted living apartment. Early in 2011, Delmar's Alzheimer's disease took a turn for the worse and there was no other choice; he had to go to a nursing home. The assisted living apartment could no longer meet Delmar's needs. My grandma, refusing to leave his side, moved with him.

When I arrived back in North Platte after Dylan's wrestling meet, I found my way to their nursing home. This was the first time I visited since they moved into the home. It was heartbreaking. Lining the hallway by the entrance, many old men and women sat in their wheelchairs staring out the window, starved for attention and saying hi to anyone in hopes that they would stop to talk. I walked down the hallway until I found Grandma and Delmar's small hospital-like room.

Grandma was still in very good health for ninety-one and was delighted to see me. She showed me the Christmas tree she decorated and placed on the desk. It only stood fifteen inches tall and was sparsely decorated with tinsel with an angel on the top. She was quick to point out the ornament on the tree that I sent her years back. I know she spent the better part of eight years worrying about me working in law enforcement, but she was always proud and displayed the pictures I sent her of me in my uniform.

I visited with her for hours as she held Delmar's hand in the chair next to her. Delmar was unconcerned with our conversation and me. I was unsure he even knew anyone else was in the room. When it came time for their dinner, I walked them down to the cafeteria holding Delmar, ensuring he wouldn't fall. As I sat Delmar down in his assigned chair, it was as if a moment of clarity came over him. He glanced at me with a surprised look and teary eyes and exclaimed, "Hey! You're back! Where have you been?"

"I've been in Arizona," I responded trying to hold back my own tears.

"Well, I've missed you," he said. Then it was over. Delmar stared blankly across the room and didn't say another word.

Grandma and I resumed our conversation for a while longer before I bade them goodnight. I knew I'd see them at my parents' house for Christmas.

The next few days before Christmas were spent helping my parents around their house and visiting my other set of grandparents in the tiny town of Tryon, Nebraska. My grandparents were ranchers, and despite being ninety-two, my Grandpa Connell was still taking care of the cows. At a young age, he acquired and worked on the ranch that his dad started. Before selling the property to a family friend, Grandpa's ranch had been his or his "papa's" since 1884. The new owner of the ranch promised Grandpa that he could still work the cattle as long as he wanted to though. In an age where people are rioting for the right to retire as soon as possible, seeing a man fight to work as long as he can is as refreshing as it is rare.

The week passed by quickly and before long it was Christmas Day. Missing so many Christmases since I moved, it felt nice to spend that day with my family. The holiday was celebrated at my parents' house, and besides my sister Shannon and her family, who live in

Maryland, everyone was there. My brother, Rod, who is nine years my elder and the oldest sibling, came with his wife, their kids and grandkids. My sister Pam and her husband, Shane, picked up Grandma and Delmar from their home so they could join. The day was filled with many laughs and stories from the past, but Delmar spent the day sitting in a rocking chair with my parents' Chihuahua on his lap in complete silence.

Time passed too quickly. Grandma began to grow weary after dinner and socializing and she was set to go home and rest. I was packing to leave early the next morning to return to Tucson. The day was spent worrying about how Delmar would react when it came time to leave. He had grown impatient and became combative the last few occasions when people took him on car rides. This time was no different. As I assisted him to the door, it was as if a switch flipped and he was ready to fight. The man who had been my grandpa for the last twenty-three years was now standing in my parents' living room punching me. He took one swing at me and almost fell over. I caught him in time to help him regain his balance, and then he swung again. This sequence of events occurred repeatedly over the course of the next couple minutes.

Finally, Delmar calmed down and we were able to coach him into the car. I hugged Grandma good-bye and they drove off with a billow of dust behind them. The disease had made him a shell of the great man he once was and for some reason this lit a fire within me; I couldn't wait to get back on the mats. We take so many things in life for granted and seldom think there will come a time our minds and bodies will fail us. I wanted to leave my mark where I could and became impatient to help outfit George with the tools he needed in his upcoming fight.

CHAPTER 4: BACK TO THE MATS

Upon my return from Nebraska, all my concentration and spare time was invested in preparing George. When I wasn't training with him, I was researching better strategies to handle certain positions and situations he was likely to encounter. My mind was constantly fixated on what I could do to help him win.

The year 2012 greeted me with hard work in the gym. Over the course of the next month, George was completely focused on the fight. He woke up early for strength and conditioning and then finished the day training in the gym. George was grinding every second. Some days it was evident the physical and mental strains were taking a toll on him.

Training for a fight is a delicate process. A fighter wants his mental and physical peak to hit at the precise moment of the match. This, however, is not a simple task. When training rigorously for an event the competitor is anxious about, it is easy for him to overtrain at the beginning. Athletes are oftentimes nervous about showing up to a fight in peak condition or about making weight. This can cause them to overtrain or not eat enough, which leads to the exhaustion of his body, mind, or both by the time of the fight. On the other hand, not training enough or overeating can cause a fighter to show up out of shape, overweight or be mentally unprepared. Obviously, arriving for a fight and feeling incapable of sustaining a rigorous pace throughout the contest can lead to serious complications. All of these aspects have to be pondered when training for a fight.

This became a concern for us. Brandon and I were worried in late December that George might be overtraining for the fight. Early on, George would leave the workout in low spirits, disappointed with his performance. When this happened, I reminded him to get the bad days out of the way and not to dwell on it. Other nights, it was apparent that no matter how much his mind was focused on training, his body wasn't at one hundred percent, as he had been battling some nerve damage in his back. There was also a concern about George's weight being too light too early. While George never came down to the fight weight of 145 pounds, he occasionally dropped to 150 pounds. These problems, however, were rare and always seemed to work themselves out. No matter how George's workout had gone the night before, he would show up the next day psyched-up to go again.

We spent forty-five days concentrating on all the scenarios we envisioned happening during the fight. Since George was coming to Boxing Inc. to work his ground game, we didn't spar on the nights he trained there. George would often work four or five rounds of focus mitts with his striking coach, and then join us on the mats. Many of the nights we worked on specific situations or positions. For example, after watching the videos, it was obvious when Cub was taken down and placed on his back, he countered with a combination of the wrestler's switch (to escape from the position), a guillotine (a choke) and a kimura (a bent armlock submission). To prepare for this, we set up in the exact same position and Chris, Jay, Brandon, and I would mimic the same attacks Cub would utilize. Once he successfully escaped, George took our backs, neutralized the position, or passed our guards; then we would start over.

The intensity increased the closer we approached fight day. As time progressed, George's challenging days became less frequent to the point where he dominated everyone he trained with. His punches were crisp, his escapes were effortless, and his positioning was solid. The week before we left for Chicago, George was a beast in the gym and ready for his fight.

"You know, I really appreciate all your help, bro," George said during one of our last training days in Tucson. "Man, I really feel like if I don't win this fight…they're gonna cut me, dude."

"Well that isn't happening," I reassured him. "You're going to destroy this guy."

"I think so too, dude."

The UFC first started in 1993. It has progressed immensely since UFC 1. Mixed Martial Arts has grown into a billion dollar business. It was because of this that I was under the impression the sport had become very sophisticated. However, I was learning that the athletic commissions were not much more organized than a pick-up basketball game at the park. Days before we were scheduled to leave, the athletic commission contacted us, stating we were now required to take a second exam in order to be licensed cornermen in Illinois, in addition to the background paperwork and passport photo. When I was notified of the exam I was impressed by the notion of requiring educated people cage-side. Then I received a copy of the multiple-choice test, which brought me to the conclusion the commission was the least educated of everyone involved. The test consisted of ridiculous questions involving such minutia as the use of "standing eight counts" (which have never been used in mixed martial arts).

Prior to the test, it was mandatory to send in our application, which contained nothing more than biographical data. The commission however, repeatedly claimed they did not have the applications. This progressed until the UFC eventually took our paperwork and sent them to the commission themselves. Right before we were scheduled to leave for the fight, history repeated itself, and the UFC told us the commission never received our exams either, even though I tried calling and sent multiple emails, to which they never responded. Fortunately, I was able to get the exam to the UFC who took care of delivering it to the commission. It was apparent even before we arrived in Chicago that it was amateur hour at the Illinois Athletic Commission.

CHAPTER 5: JANUARY 24TH

I told George and Ed I would meet them at the airport so we could fly together. I lived on the other side of town from them and it made no sense for us to drive to the airport together. Pierre could not make the trip with us and planned to travel to Chicago later in the week.

Early on the morning of Tuesday, January 24th, I arrived at Tucson International Airport. Breezing through check-in and security, I had time to kill before boarding so I sat in the terminal playing on my phone. Before I realized the time, I noticed our flight beginning to board and George and Ed were nowhere to be found. I started to wonder if we were flying together. I was fairly certain when I ordered my tickets a few weeks ago that we were on the same flight, but I began to second-guess myself. I texted George, asking his whereabouts and informed him the plane was boarding. Soon, I looked up and noticed all passengers on our flight were boarded. I quickly ran up to the attendant and notified her two more people were showing up. She said they only had a couple minutes, and the flight was running late and needed to leave.

Right then, George texted and said they were passing through security. When they finally arrived at the gate, they were being escorted by a gentleman, who had hooked them up with free food from one of the vendors. "They ain't gonna leave us, dude", George said as they walked up. We were the last ones to board the plane.

After a brief layover in Dallas, we landed in Chicago that afternoon and walked to baggage claim. Next to our baggage carousel was a man holding a Zuffa sign. We grabbed our bags, hopped on the bus and headed into town. The trip from the airport to the hotel was brutal. After traveling all day and sitting on the plane for so long, the hour-long trip into the city, in Chicago traffic, was the last thing we wanted to endure.

We drove up to the Hard Rock Hotel in downtown Chicago and the circus began. As soon as we stepped off the bus, a few fans began taking pictures and asking for autographs. We then stood in line and waited to check into our room. One of the hotel attendants asked us to place our bags in a back room, for safekeeping and informed us to go upstairs with Burt.

Before the trip, I was under the naïve impression that Dana White personally oversaw UFC events. I didn't expect him to be fully involved with the fighters, especially the undercard fighters, but I did expect him to be present and direct orders. I was wrong. Burt Watson ran the show. Burt was a middle-aged, medium-built black man. He was the production manager for the UFC and the man in charge of getting everything done from organizing weigh-ins to verifying everyone was where they needed to be when they needed to be there. The entire time we were in Chicago, if there was a place to be, Burt was there. If there was an issue, Burt was taking care of it. If there was a person to talk to, Burt was that guy. He was responsible for the high-quality shows that the UFC puts on. Listening to Burt's motivational tirades made *me* want to fight!

We followed Burt up two flights of stairs into one of the hotel's conference rooms. The room was transformed into a training area, one of two mat rooms. Each room posted a list of fighters who were allowed to train in that particular room. Half the fighters' names were on the door of each room. This allowed the fighters to train there for the week without worrying about their opponents walking in to see what they were working on. Each room had mats laid out on the floor, a mountain of towels, and a scale for the fighters to weigh themselves.

Burt led us into the training room and asked each fighter to step on the scale. He recorded the fighters' weights when they arrived. Burt was on top of every little detail. One of the fighters who weighed in alongside George showed up twenty pounds over. Burt was less than impressed, but he simply said, "You're a professional. I expect you know what you need to do."

After the weight check, we followed Burt into another conference room filled with people. Many of those present were behind computers typing online bios for the fighters; others were ensuring the Illinois State Athletic Commission's licensing paperwork was properly filled out for each fighter and each of the fighter's seconds, the official term for cornermen. While we were in this room, all fighters were obligated to each sign 180 event posters. As one could imagine, this was a lengthy and boring process. Two or three fighters would gather around a table surrounding a giant stack of 32"x48" posters. They would sign each poster, then slide that poster back so they could autograph the next in the stack. It was an excruciating task for everyone. Many fighters arrived to the hotel tired and hungry and signing memorabilia was the last task any of them wanted to do.

After completing the poster signing, we returned to the lobby to check into our hotel room. Once we arrived to our room, we relaxed for a bit while watching the State of the Union Address. The President's speech immediately fueled the room with political questions. My upbringing steered me more toward conservatism than most people in Southern Arizona. Ed was by far the most liberal in the group. I learned a long time ago that arguing about politics was a waste of energy. I'm not sure if anyone in the history of politics has ever changed their view based on a conversation they had with someone from another party. No matter how hard Ed tried to drag me into a serious conversation about taxes, wars or abortion, I wouldn't take the bait. I just smiled and answered with a short yes or no.

The room offered two queen-sized beds and for me, a rollaway bed crammed in the entryway. Ed noticed a rather disturbing picture displayed on the wall. This was photo art of an unfamiliar-man in his fifties. The picture was a close-up of his face with a very peculiar expression. Hung at the foot of one of the beds, I can assure this was not a face one wanted to wake up to in the morning.

"Who the hell would put this in a room where people sleep?" exclaimed Ed. "I'm ripping this thing down." After failing to remove it—it was secured to the wall with screws—Ed found a spare blanket in the room and covered it instead.

While Ed was fussing about the picture, George was surfing the internet. Wanting to make plans for the upcoming week before the fight, George said, "Hey, Joe Rogan is doing a comedy show in that theatre down the street, dude!" Joe Rogan is not only a stand-up comedian, but he has hosted popular TV shows like *Fear Factor* and *The Man Show*. Rogan has also been a longtime color commentator for the UFC and has an extensive martial arts background, including a black belt in jiu jitsu. George then sent Rogan a message to inquire about purchasing tickets to the show.

"I'm not going to that show!" Ed shouted. "If I go, I'm going to heckle him, but I'm not going anyway, so it doesn't matter."

George and I laughed because we knew why Ed was being so defiant. In one of George's previous fights, the camera was in his corner after the first round and the audio picked up Ed advising George. During the interaction, trying to build up his confidence, Ed told George "You won that round." despite in most people's eyes, George lost the round. After hearing this, Rogan, the UFC's commentator, ridiculed Ed, stating, "I don't know what fight that guy is watching!" Ed took this to heart and hadn't forgiven Rogan for it.

After hanging out in the room, we went downstairs to the conference room where mats were set up for workouts. Michael Bisping was working on his takedown defense when we walked in. This was the first time I had to tell myself that I needed to stay professional. Bisping was one of the UFC's biggest stars and was fighting in the co-main event. The last thing I wanted to do was to make it look like George brought a bunch of star-struck amateurs with him, even though in my case it was the truth.

Bisping was the first British star in MMA and became a polarizing persona from his appearance on an earlier season of *The Ultimate Fighter* reality show. Many fans base their feelings about fighters on the fighter's attitude portrayed on the show. Bisping adopted a reputation of being a little obnoxious on television. This reputation followed him throughout his career. However, over the course of the weekend, I discovered he was one of the more personable fighters on the card.

We shared the mats with Bisping. I kept time while Ed held focus mitts for George on one end of the mat. Bisping and his crew worked on takedown defense and focus mitts on the other end. After George finished hitting the mitts, he and Ed wrestled, and Bisping and his crew sat around, talked, and half-heartedly watched them roll (a term in jiu jitsu used to refer to wrestling practice). George then executed a technique to take his opponent's back, a move I had taught him right before the Hioki fight. Taking the back means getting behind your opponent and essentially becoming a human backpack. This is a dominant position in jiu jitsu and similarly a very effective position in MMA as well. Being behind your opponent can have many offensive advantages, such as angles to strike, chokes to apply, or the ability to transition to armlocks. In spite of that, the biggest advantage and my favorite part of the position is the difficulty for your opponent to land any effective strikes. As soon as George took the back, I overheard Bisping compliment the move and say he hadn't seen it before. The comment, however small, gave me a feeling of legitimacy in a room filled with some of the most elite fighters on the planet.

After training, we were even hungrier than when we arrived and headed to McDonald's for a bite. As we walked up to the restaurant, a teenager was closing the door and locking up. George ran up and asked if we could order. The kid wasn't going to let him in. George then asked him, "Hey, do you know what the UFC is?" and the kid smiled.

"I'll give you free tickets to the UFC fight this weekend if you let us in to eat."

The UFC gives fighters a certain amount of tickets to the show. The bigger a draw you are, the better the tickets and the more tickets you get. The tickets are for the fighters to give to their family, sell for extra money, or to watch the fights after their own. For this fight, George was given four, since the only people from Tucson who came to watch George were going to be in his corner; George decided early on that he would give the tickets to fans. This was his chance to do so.

The young McDonald's worker looked at George, shook his head no, locked the door and walked away.

We all laughed in disbelief. George just tried to barter UFC tickets for the opportunity to buy McDonald's food. I was in shock. What kind of kid would pass up the chance for free tickets to a UFC event?

We found a sandwich shop down the street and picked up something a little tastier and certainly a lot healthier than McDonald's.

Back at the hotel, right before killing the lights, George piped up and said "Sweet! Rogan is going to hook us up with tickets to the show! He just IM'd me on Twitter."

"I ain't going to watch the show even if it is free!" Ed exclaimed, but we knew he would go.

CHAPTER 6: JANUARY 25ᵀᴴ

I never imagined a hotel rollaway bed could ever be so comfortable. We slept in until 10 a.m. and then George and I got dressed and walked to a Dunkin Donuts down the street. My body was craving caffeine and required it to make it through the morning. George was not a coffee drinker, but decided he would try a small cup.

We returned to the hotel room and woke Ed up; he would have slept all day if we hadn't. While sitting in the hotel room and enjoying the coffee, the conversation took a serious turn. A show on television highlighted some young kids who had been involved in gangs and were now in juvenile detention. We discussed how easy it was for young people to get caught up in the wrong crowd. We each gave accounts about our younger days and how we made mistakes regarding the people we associated with and the choices we made.

Ed surprised me. He revealed to us that he used his trials and errors from his youth to be a positive influence on the younger generation. On a regular basis, Ed was a guest speaker at schools and various organizations to encourage kids to make smart life choices. I was impressed. After knowing Ed for a few years, I knew he was an extremely caring guy, but it surprised me to hear of his hidden depths.

"These kids don't get it," Ed said, "They sit there and try to talk tough, saying they're born into it. Like being a gangster in Tucson is an inescapable life."

"That's how it feels, dude. They don't realize how ridiculous it is." George told us about things he had done as a youth. I guessed some things correctly, but to hear his story opened my eyes.

He said, "Dude, I can remember feeling like there was no way out of hangin' with the guys I was hangin' with."

Fighting has a unique way of bringing people together who would normally not associate with one another. Growing up close to the U.S./Mexico Border can bring about its own challenges. Many people are influenced and seduced by the idea of earning "easy money" by running drugs, transporting illegal aliens or both. It's simple for young people to fall in with the wrong crowd. During his younger years, George had fallen in with the wrong friends, the wrong influences and the wrong environment. By the time George was in his late teens, he had frequent run-ins with the Tucson police and was quickly spiraling out of control.

I, on the other hand, grew up with no major problems. My home life growing up was the Mayberry-type story. I was a decent high school athlete, on the drama team and was homecoming king. I went to college, graduated in four and a half years, and landed a good job by the age of twenty-four.

Our paths were in sharp contrast of one another and only crossed because of Brazilian Jiu Jitsu. Though our lives started much differently, there we were hanging out at the Hard Rock Hotel on Michigan Avenue preparing for a nationally-televised sporting event. This was a thought I never would have imagined seven years ago.

Friendships like ours are not uncommon in the MMA or jiu-jitsu world. The mats, cage, and ring are unique environments. On the mats there are no religions, politics, sexes, background checks, or financial statuses. I have seen Muslims train with Christians, cops with felons, Democrats with Republicans, and country club "gentry" with trailer park "trash". In the gym we are all there for the common purpose of making each other better, and while doing so a unique bond is created. George, Ed and I were no different. We grew up with markedly different backgrounds and opportunities, but we sacrificed our time and effort to make others better, no matter how unlike us they were. Perhaps that is why we had similar feelings towards the kids on television. We knew their potential was greater than they could imagine. Their lives could change directions instantly with a slight change of attitude and company.

Most of the fighters on the card were busy shooting video for the production of the show on Saturday. Luckily, Burt told George he didn't need to film because they were using file footage from his previous fights. This meant we had the entire day to explore, and we wanted to see this freezing city, which stood in such sharp contrast with sunny Tucson.

As we walked out of the hotel, I was challenged again to not be a fan and to try to be professional. As a jiu jitsu guy, there are certainly some fighters and some fighters' styles I admire more than others. The moment we stepped out onto the sidewalk, we ran into one of my favorite fighters, Demian Maia. Maia began his career in the UFC with a bang, submitting and dominating fights with his superior jiu jitsu. In one fight, he won in the first round without throwing a single punch. That fight made a huge impact on me. Now here he was, standing three feet in front of me, having a conversation with George. I've learned over the years that oftentimes you can be disappointed when meeting someone you really admire. This was not the case with Maia. He was an unbelievably nice man who greeted everyone with a smile.

As we walked away from Maia, fans were hitting up the fighters for autographs. Over the course of the week, the hotel was inundated with autograph seekers. These guys were dedicated. The hotel forced them to leave the lobby, so instead they stood in the chilling zero-degree streets of Chicago waiting for fighters to exit the buildings. Many of the autograph seekers had 8 ½ by 11-inch photographs of the fighters and were asking for the fighters' signatures. Two fans approached George and asked him to sign some photos. The first guy began handing George the photos, and George started signing. I paid little attention at first, but eventually Ed and I realized George was signing photos of someone else. I didn't recognize the fighter in the photo, but it was a skinny white guy, so it was close but no cigar. By the time we noticed, George was done signing six or seven of the first guy's photos. The second fan began handing George the same photographs, but I couldn't let it happen again so I brought it to their attention. Everyone was mildly embarrassed. George felt bad he hadn't really looked at the photo, and the fans were embarrassed they hadn't recognized the correct fighter.

"I thought I was signing a picture of you, dude!" George joked with him.

After straightening out the autographs, we walked up Michigan Avenue. Living in Arizona, we were accustomed to long stretches of open desert and spread-out cities so we appreciated the vertical city next to the lake. The prominent skyscrapers dominating the city's skylines and the art-deco and modern architecture differed substantially from the Southwest style. It wasn't just the city. The dress attire of Chicago was more refined and fashion-forward, with structured and sophisticated styles. Locals were much more serious and walked with a purpose and spoke with certainty. The city and its people fascinated us.

Michigan Avenue was beyond amazing. I visited Chicago before, but I never had the liberty to explore that area of the city. We roamed from shop to shop searching for gifts for our girlfriends back home. George was engaged to be married in the spring. Ed was dating a girl who was a fighter as well and whom he met while training.

I was still dating Bernice. Within a couple months she planned to move from Phoenix to Tucson. It was a huge step for me since I have never lived with a girlfriend before, but I had few reservations. She was an incredible fit for me and I can say I have never met a more beautiful and extraordinary girl. Occasionally, I hear old men speak about their wives, saying their wives brought out the best in them. I always dismissed the notion as old people romanticizing about their lives to make them feel better about themselves. After being with Bernice, however, I could honestly say she did bring out the best in me. While in Chicago, I felt guilty about being on trip without her. She loves traveling and I knew she wanted to travel to Chicago with us, but in the end, the trip was more business than leisure.

After exploring the city and buying gifts for our girls, it was time to hit the gym again. We returned to the second floor mat room at the hotel. George and Ed worked focus mitts for four rounds.

Then we spent the remainder of the time game planning terminology for the fight. The terminology was designed to communicate with George during the fight. The key was to make the code words simple enough so when even in the heat of the moment, your fighter could still decipher your commands, yet keep the opponent unaware of what you were saying.

Deciding on the terms was easier than expected. Since we had been training together for so long, certain words already had a common meaning. We used them for specific commands for this fight. For instance, utilizing George's reach was imperative, like it was in the fight George had against Dave Kaplan in UFC 98. One strategy George used to keep Kaplan away was to throw long, straight punches. We would shout "David" to instruct George to repeatedly throw jabs to prevent Cub from closing the distance.

The training session went well. George was smooth in every aspect. His punches were hard, making the loud "pop" as they struck the focus mitts. His footwork was efficient and quick. His kicks were powerful. We left the mat room feeling confident George was peaking at the right time.

CHAPTER 7: JANUARY 26TH

Bright and early on Thursday, I woke up and headed straight to Dunkin for my morning coffee. I returned to see George pumped up for the fight. He was visualizing the match, preparing himself for anything that could happen. He was full of energy and ready to duel.

After we rousted Ed, we walked down Michigan Avenue in search of food. Two Chicago police officers were kind enough to steer us in the right direction to a nice little eatery at the corner of an office building. The place was crawling with people in expensive suits, while we were dressed in jeans, hoodies and beanies. We received a few odd looks.

While eating, Ed talked about the bad luck he had with managers over the years. "Dude, I had to get a new manager. I wasn't getting any fights." Ed had been fighting for quite some time. The first card I saw him at was Rage in Cage in 2005, defending his lightweight title. Even then it was obvious he possessed more talent than anyone else fighting. Since that time, I always wondered why he wasn't given more fights. Despite recent fights in Bellator and the IFL, where he fought way out of his weight class, Ed had not fought as often as he wanted to. In fact, he went a whole year without one match. "The only fight I got that whole year was a fight that I found myself; that guy never even got me any sponsors," Ed explained, referring to his manager. "He couldn't get me in any bigger shows and no one in the local shows would fight me."

"Well, dude, in your next fight I'll sponsor you," I told Ed. I was just in the beginning process of launching my combat sports training log company, Fight Log Media, and the timing of Ed's fight was going to work perfectly.

"Hell yeah," Ed answered. "You got a deal."

I was excited for the chance to have my company's name on national television at a Bellator event. Obtaining good marketing for my business would be a big challenge. I did not have a big name in the fighting scene nor did I have the funds to pay a celebrity to push the product for me. I started Fight Log Media and launched the Fightlogs.com website with a $4,000 dollar tax return. After George's fight with Hioki, I could see the benefit of utilizing deliberate practice. Our training of drilling specific positions repeatedly had an impact on George's ability to thwart Hioki's offense from the mount position. I wanted to strategize a way to help other fighters design their own training programs for their upcoming fights or for overall improvement.

Over the previous couple years I became a dedicated reader of books focused on topics of maximizing human potential. Many of these books shared common themes. One such theme was if you can't track a behavior, you can't improve upon it; we need metrics to track our progress. In martial arts, metrics are difficult to measure since any given technique has many variables (your level of fitness, skill, the fitness and skill of your opponent, the position you use a technique from, etc.).

Following the Hioki match I worked nightly designing training journals to guide a fighter at any level to incorporate the principles of the Self-Regulated Learning paradigm designed by Psychologist Dr. Barry Zimmeran. Self-Regulated Learning encompasses a cycle of three stages: The Forethought Phase (Goal Setting), The Performance Phase (Self-Recording), and The Self-Reflection Phase (Self-Evaluation and Adaptation). I spent countless hours designing the best platform for my idea. After a couple months I had a valuable journal that enabled fighters to record metrics, utilize Self-Regulated Learning, and keep a journal of daily training. I was ready to kick off Fight Log Media.

The company was going to be challenging to market. Not many companies produced these types of journals. I also didn't know if there was a demand for them.

Still at the restaurant, we chatted about game planning and strategizing for fights. I explained to Ed and George about the CARVER method, an approach used by the military and other governmental groups, to prioritize not only a fight game plan, but as a means to prioritize a fighter's training leading up to the fight. The CARVER method is a matrix style that helps put numerical values to strategies in order to create an effective plan that produces the desired result. This matrix places a numerical value on a category based on six criteria: Criticality, Accessibility, Recuperability, Vulnerability, Effect, and Recognizability. Using the CARVER method makes assigning values to the many variables of the fight game possible, and thus turns training into a science rather than an art.

During the Vietnam War, the U.S. military developed a risk-based assessment matrix to help prioritize enemy targets. This assessment became the CARVER matrix. Today, many law enforcement and emergency personnel utilize this method when creating agency strategies.

Here is a breakdown on what each CARVER element means when using it for MMA:

Criticality	Is it critical that I use it to win the fight?
Accessibility	Is this accessible? (Am I able to do this?)
Recuperability	Will my opponent be able to recover from this? How easily or quickly will he recover?
Vulnerability	Is my opponent vulnerable in this area?
Effect	What is the psychological/physical impact of

	accomplishing this?
Recognizability	Will the judges recognize the advantage or strike?

To set up the matrix, you would create a spreadsheet similar to the one you see below. After reviewing film on your opponent's fights, consult with your coaches or training partners and write down four to eight areas to focus on when training for the fight. Then rate all positions or areas of training in every CARVER category by scoring each 1-5 (5 being the most critical, the most accessible, the hardest to recover from, the most vulnerable, the biggest impact, and very recognizable; 1 being the least).

Rating these areas can be done statistically by compiling careful statistics of your opponent's last three fights. Having your coach and training partners create their own matrix for your fight and compare them with your own can be helpful. This will give you a less biased view and give yourself ideas you may not have thought of.

Below is a sample CARVER matrix of what a Muay Thai-dominant fighter (a striker) might formulate if he is competing against a wrestler who likes to utilize the cage for dirty boxing.

THE CARVER MATRIX

	Escaping from the guard	Takedowns	Single Leg Defense	Boxing	Escaping against the fence	Passing the Guard
Criticality	4	2	5	4	4	1
Accessibility	4	2	4	4	3	1
Recuperability	2	1	2	3	3	2
Vulnerability	4	1	2	3	2	3
Effect	4	5	5	3	3	4
Recognizability	2	4	4	4	4	4
Total	20	15	22	21	19	15

Utilizing the above matrix can give a fighter the direction that training cage work and takedown defense is more important than drilling single legs and guard passing. Again, by adding quantitative data to a problem, the solution is easier to identify and it is a solution based on science, not gut feeling.

I discussed with George and Ed how the matrix worked and how it could help improve coaching and preparing for fights. Although most fighters may already do this in some fashion, this was a more scientific approach to it. Afterwards, I felt a little foolish telling two professional fighters how to game plan their fights.

Following breakfast, we set out to take in more of Chicago. We agreed it would be fun to find an old prohibition-era speakeasy. Within walking distance we discovered a place called The Green Door. Giddy like little kids, we became stoked to check it. After a thirty-minute walk, we found it. It was a corner tavern that instantly depicted its age and character. The crooked, forward-leaning door revealed the hardships the building endured through past years. The floors were wood with a rustic charm. Years of spilled beer and foot traffic gave the wood floor its own personality while the walls were covered with Guinness signs and old photographs of the city. Just by walking in you could feel the spirit of good times. I immediately wanted a beer, but we were in town for other reasons.

George weighed in the next day, and even though he was right on schedule to make weight, eating was out of the question. Bar food was the last thing he needed. Normally I would never dream of eating in front of someone who was cutting weight. Having to cut weight for tournaments myself, I understood that insatiable feeling of watching others eat, but Ed and I were starving and each ordered a sandwich anyway. While eating, we asked the waitress if we could see the speakeasy. She was reluctant to give us a tour of the old bar because they were understaffed. Knowing our window of opportunity was rapidly closing, I spoke up and clued her in on the reason we were in Chicago in the first place. Without delay, the tone of the conversation changed. She told us the manager would take us to see the hidden room.

Promptly, a short-statured gentleman with a shaved head approached the table. He asked, "So you guys want to see the speakeasy?" We jumped up in anticipation before he finished his sentence. He led us down narrow stairs to a "T" in the stairway, unlocked a door and we walked in. The speakeasy was a dark room, sixteen feet wide and thirty-two feet in length with a long wooden bar on the right and a slightly raised stage at the other end. To the left was a closet filled with aged bottles of liquor, with red drapes hanging on both sides. The manager told us the room was uncovered in the 1970's during a building remodel.

We were standing in a unique piece of American History. Maybe Al Capone was even in that room at one point. Sadly, the manager informed us the room had been broken into and burglarized the weekend before our visit. Much of the original décor and relics of the hideout were now gone. We snapped a few pictures and made our way back upstairs.

As we walked to our hotel, I reached for my phone, but it was gone. In an instant, I was in a panic. Losing my cell phone with every number of all my friends with no backup was a terrible feeling. I used the phone to call KJ five minutes earlier; we knew it couldn't be far. George and I began to backtrack, asking people on the street if they had seen a phone. Ed called it in the hopes we might hear it ring.

George and I retraced our steps towards The Green Door until we came to the spot where I last had my phone. It was nowhere to be found. We looked for half an hour until I finally gave up and ended the search. George and I returned to where Ed had been calling the line.

"Who's your boy?" Ed called out.

"Did you find it?" I inquired.

"No dude, but some chick just picked up and said she would meet us on this corner."

We waited for what seemed like forever, wondering if she would truly bring the phone. Soon, an attractive young lady was walking straight towards us. She was petite, but athletically built. "Did you lose your phone?" she asked.

"I owe you so much!" I said.

We thanked her for bringing the phone and I tried giving her money, but she refused and said, "You're supposed to do one good deed a day, so I guess I'm done for the day."

We began making small talk and it turned out Abigail was a ballerina at the Joffrey Ballet Hall, which was close to the Hard Rock Hotel. George still had tickets for the fight, and he asked if she was interested in the tickets as a reward for returning the phone. She agreed, and I took her number and told her we would meet her the next day to give her the tickets.

For some reason or another, this weird chain of events shot a bolt of energy through the three of us. We went from the emotional low of losing my phone to being energetic and laughing and joking like teenagers.

We stopped by a restaurant where George picked up a salad. Back at the room, George stepped on the scale: 155 pounds. We were twenty-four hours away from weigh-ins and George was ten pounds over the 145-pound weight class. George was concerned he was slightly over his target weight, so it was time to hit the mat room.

Losing ten pounds in twenty-four hours may sound like a superhuman feat for people who have never done so. Wrestlers and fighters know all too well that it's possible, but far from fun. The human body is composed mainly of water. A person can change their weight over a short period of time by manipulating the amount of water in the body. A fighter can drop the weight by sweating and by limiting water intake. Although it's not a healthy or practical way to lose weight permanently, it is common practice for fighters since they only need to be at a certain weight at the weigh-ins. Hitting the mat room was going to help drop water that night and burn calories.

Upon entering the mat room, I saw one of the most intimidating men I have ever seen. We watched this enormously muscular man hammer the mitts like a professional boxer. He hit fast and moved his feet faster. Despite being around football nearly all of my life and knowing very gifted and powerful athletes, I had never seen a man that big move that well. George, Ed and I watched this guy work and then looked at each other sheepishly.

After ending his workout, he and his crew introduced themselves. His name was Lavar Johnson. Johnson fought for Strikeforce, another leading MMA promotional company, prior to being bought out by Zuffa. He was a kind, well-spoken, sociable man with a nasty-looking scar across his stomach that ran from his lower chest down the center of his abdomen. In the middle of the conversation, Ed asked, "How did you get the scar? Did you get shot?"

"I'd shoot you too!" George piped up without missing a beat or waiting for a response.

Lavar laughed and went on to tell us he was shot at a family gathering a few years earlier, when someone opened fire on the crowd. Lavar and his corner stuck around chatting. Although I had never seen him fight before, he had been on Strikeforce fight cards. I became a fan right away.

It was our turn to train. George drilled five hard five-minute rounds on the mitts. Then we switched to grappling, working on the same positions we ingrained in his mind and body over the last forty-five days. George was performing flawlessly and smoothly. It was obvious George was peaking at the correct time. He had prepared properly for the fight.

That evening, Pierre arrived in Chicago. This was the first time we met but we had plenty in common and hit it off well. Pierre was George's fianceé's sister's husband—essentially his brother in-law. He never fought before but was a great friend of George, and after visiting with him for a while it was clear why George liked him. Pierre was constantly cracking jokes and keeping the mood light, which is important when you have a guy in the room that was "angry hungry" from cutting weight.

CHAPTER 8: WEIGH-INS

My eyes slowly opened as the early morning sun peeked in through the curtains on Friday. It was going to be a hectic and busy day. Cutting weight is no easy task, so I made it my mission to make the weight cut as painless as possible for George.

The hotel phone rang first thing in the morning. The front desk clerk notified George that his fight shorts, walk-out shirts and banner arrived. We needed to meet for weigh-ins in the hotel at 3:00 p.m., so we had work to do.

Any apparel a fighter wears during a UFC event must be cleared. The UFC has a list of sponsors who cannot be affiliated with UFC events, for one reason or another. They also charge a sponsorship fee to be associated with their events. To ensure an unauthorized logo is not placed on anyone's sponsor banner or shorts, Burt and his crew inspect them. This particular event was the first that no longer allowed sponsorship from gun, knife, or outdoor supply companies. Earlier in the week, George indicated this made a large impact on the amount of money he could earn for the fight. One of his biggest sponsors was a firearms company, and the ban on such short notice did not provide him ample time to find sponsors to replace them. The late and seemingly unnecessary decision to prohibit these companies was costing George serious money.

Following the clothing and banner inspection, it was time to cut weight. The UFC provided fighters and their crews free passes to L.A. Fitness a block away from the hotel. Nearly every fighter there would be using the sauna for the weight cut. Fighters utilize the sauna to dehydrate themselves and cut water weight. The humidity in the sauna causes the fighter to sweat excessively, depleting the body's water.

Ed sat in the sauna with George to keep him company during the weight cut. Pierre and I stood by guarding the gear and kept time. The best way to utilize this type of weight cutting is to break the time in the sauna into small increments. Too much time in the room at once is as mentally exhausting as it is physically draining. When one of George's sauna sessions was at its end, I opened the door. The 12x12 room was packed with about fifteen fighters and trainers who all looked miserable.

"Time, George," I said.

"Shut the door!" someone shouted.

I looked over and there was Marc Fiore yelling at me. Fiore trained with and was a cornerman for one of my all-time favorite fighters, Matt Hughes. I had seen the guy on television for years and now he was shouting at me.

He was right. In a momentary lapse of judgment, I held the door open too long to tell George it was time, allowing heat to escape. This meant the fighters would be required to stay in the room longer and the sauna can be a miserable experience. I don't respond lightly to anyone yelling at me and I'm sure that was evident from the look on my face, but I remained lighthearted and shut the door.

Throughout the day, George made six trips into the sauna for a total of an hour and ten minutes. Despite losing ten pounds in less than twenty-four hours, George was in much better shape than some of the other fighters.

Chris Weidman was having an extremely hard time. He agreed to take his fight on short notice, which made the cut much more difficult. At one point he was lying on the hallway floor covered in towels with his cornermen standing around him. A few members of the gym offered to call a doctor. It was a slightly humorous sight to me. It was not humorous to watch this fighter push his body to the limits, however, it did bring to my attention that a fighter's mentality is completely deviant from the social norm. The normal reaction from most of the population when seeing their friend extremely dehydrated and lying on the floor in the middle of the hallway would be to show concern and to get help. In contrast, this fighter's corner would casually step over his teammate and only encouraged him to return to the sauna.

Scanning the locker room, I saw the sunken faces of the dehydrated athletes, and they looked miserable. These fighters had put their bodies under extreme stress. Living in the desert, I was trained to recognize the signs of dehydration and overheating to the point of needing medical attention. All of these fighters were showing the signs. But it was all part of the fighter's world.

George's weight was perfect. I was gathering our gear together and disposing the towels we used when I heard, "Hey, sorry about earlier." It was Fiore.

I smiled, laughed and said, "You don't have to apologize; you were right. I wasn't thinking."

"I hate being in the sauna. I just wanted to apologize for yelling earlier."

"Not a big deal." I responded.

The time was quickly approaching when we needed to meet for weigh-ins. I stopped at a nearby noodle shop to buy food for George for post weigh-ins. Then returned to the mat room for a meeting.

The modus operandi for the weigh-ins was hurry up and wait. The fighters and their corners met in the mat room. Burt gave us the rundown on what would take place and what to do in case a fighter did not make weight.

The room was filled with various aromas making my mouth water. Each fighter had their meals they would eat as soon as they made weight. I was starving. Even though George was the one cutting weight, I had not eaten since the early morning and we were nearing 3 p.m. On the other hand, I wasn't nearly as hungry as the fighters. The looks on their faces could only be described as "pissed off, bordering on rage". They reached a level of "angry-hungry" that was almost combustible.

Burt began calling the names of the fighters. Although the weigh-ins were held in a theatre located on the same block, we were to be bussed to the venue to protect the fighters from chaos created by fans. We filed out of the room, down the stairs, through the lobby, outside, and onto the bus. I was amazed at the number of admirers who lined up to watch the fighters exit the hotel. Fans were cheering and knew every fighter by name. Being surrounded by an excited audience watching your every move was an adrenaline rush and gave me a false sense of importance, especially considering none of them knew or cared who I was.

We exited the bus and were directed down the alley behind the theatre, through the back door, and downstairs into the basement. Half of the fighters were placed in one room and their opponents in another. The fighters were forced to endure yet another round of questioning by the Illinois Athletic Commission and a last minute physical.

Burt told us only the fighters' chief second, in George's case, Ed, was allowed to accompany the fighter at the weigh-in and the rest of us were to go watch with the audience. Pierre and I trekked our way upstairs and grabbed good seats.

The theatre was packed for the weigh-ins and the crowd was eager with anticipation. Who would have thought over a thousand people would show up to watch famished and dehydrated men strip down to their underwear and step on a scale? These events were perfectly marketed. Fans cheered for their favorite fighters and booed the fighters they hated. The music was blaring as Joe Rogan announced each fighter as they stepped onto the stage. The fighter would strip down and step on the scale, flex for the crowd then stare down their opponent, which built even more hype for their fight.

George's name was called. He stepped onto the scale and hit 145 perfectly. Then his opponent tipped the scale at the exact same weight. When George and Cub faced off, the size difference was obvious. George, who stands about 6'1", towered over the 5'7" Cub, looking down on him like Cub was a child. It was hard to tell for sure, but I imagine the size discrepancy gave Cub some pause. The difference in their reach was several inches, which would allow George to land straight punches from a safe distance, a considerable advantage in any fight.

Back at the hotel, our mission was to get George hydrated and back to feeling normal again. We spent a majority of the evening in the room making that our primary concern. Within a short time, George returned to normal weight and energy levels were as high as ever.

George received the tickets for the fights earlier in the day. While George drank water and an electrolyte replacement drink, I attempted to contact Abigail, the ballerina who found my phone, to give her the tickets we promised her. After making several calls, we failed to reach her. It seemed no one wanted the free tickets.

We returned to the theatre for the Joe Rogan comedy show. Rogan set aside some great seats for us about five rows from the stage. He had a few opening acts, including a very funny actor named Joey Diaz. Joe Rogan's show was entertaining and had us laughing and joking the remainder of the night.

After the show, we stopped to eat our second dinner for the night. We were relaxed but excited. George was pleased his weight cut was over and now all he had left was the fight. The cut is often referred to as "the fight before the fight." It is an agonizing experience but by bedtime that night George's weight returned to 160 pounds.

CHAPTER 9: FIGHT DAY

"WHOO!!! Let's do this!"

I woke up to George yelling in the hotel room. He was worked up and wired to go, as were the rest of us. After a week of eating, sleeping, talking, and dreaming this fight to death, we were ready. Although George was the one fighting, we viewed this as a team effort. We spent a lot of time helping George prepare and we were eager to watch him reap the rewards of his hard work.

However, our first concern this morning was to get a meal in our stomachs. This was going to be another long day. We treaded down the street to a place we found the night before called the South Water Café. The café was located in a basement with an inviting atmosphere and delicious food, but the breakfast was as expensive as I ever had.

Breakfast was filled with good conversation, but as usual, it turned to fighting. We discussed how lucky we considered professional fighters were nowadays compared to those who paved the way for them. We brought up unfortunate examples of fighters who still currently fought because in their prime they were not compensated as well as fighters are today. It saddened us to see how mediocre fighters were able to earn victories over once astonishing fighters simply because the legends were far past the peak of their careers.

A fighter who commonly is referenced in conversations like this is Jens Pulver. Pulver was the first Lightweight Champion in the UFC and broke ground for many smaller fighters. Since then, Pulver continued to fight and has lost to subpar opponents. To any "little guy" like Ed, George and me, Pulver is a legend and a hero. He fought much larger competitors to make his mark on the sport. Because of Jens Pulver, smaller weight classes exist in the UFC.

"I hate seeing Jens like that," George said. "That's why I gotta take care of my money. I only have so many years left of this. Hell, I might get cut tonight. You never know."

Even at the highest level, fighters don't get retirement packages or pensions like in other major athletic organizations. To my knowledge, even Pulver did not receive compensation for his pioneering work for MMA. Because most fighters typically don't fight past forty it is crucial to be financially smart and plan for their future at an early age.

In recent years, the UFC has done a better job of educating their fighters on money management and how to leverage their current salaries and statuses to help them financially in the future. As far as I know, this type of education was not available for the earlier fighters.

We also talked about training camps. George spoke about being on The Ultimate Fighter show and his stint in Las Vegas. He couldn't comprehend why people trained in famous gyms. "The great thing about being in a small gym is that when I'm preparing for a fight, everyone there is there for me. At larger gyms, you don't have people there for you; they're merely there for themselves." I never thought about that before. While prepping George for the fight, I felt like a novice, uncertain if we were doing the right things. I hadn't helped many others get ready for fights, especially one of this magnitude. I asked myself why George would select two people to be in his corner who never fought before. Now listening to George speak during breakfast, it made sense to me. He wanted to be surrounded by those he felt comfortable with in his corner. A corner's main job was to have the fighter's best interest in mind, not to give him Mr. Miyagi advice.

After breakfast, the group split up. Pierre and Ed wandered around town while George and I returned to the hotel room, which was being cleaned when we arrived. George and I found a quiet lobby on the second floor of the hotel. There were only two chairs in the lobby, without another soul around.

Immediately, the conversation turned to the fight and the plan. George needed to use his size and reach advantage to frustrate Cub. On tape, we perceived Cub had a tendency to become impatient and start moving straight forward and throw big overhand rights with his head down.

We discussed the possibility of Cub shooting in to take George down in order to negate the reach difference. From watching fight footage, we recognized Cub's primary takedown was a hip toss. He commonly used it to make a statement and not necessarily to utilize a top game, but we pondered if Cub would try to catch us by surprise by shooting in making George fight off his back like Hioki had done in the second round of George's last fight. This scenario didn't worry us a great deal though since George has agile takedown defense, but it was a possibility.

After our brief "what if" session we made our way to the room. The match was deep in George's head, and he spent his time shadowboxing in the elevator, the lobby, the hallway, and anywhere else he found himself. George was mentally prepared for the fight.

As George, Ed and Pierre waited in the room for the time to head to the arena, I decided to dispose of the two extra tickets, since George's manager took the other two. I trekked down to the lobby and was lucky enough to find another fighter who could use them. His camp brought more people than they had tickets for and needed extra seats. I found it humorous we couldn't give the tickets away, but we were able to sell them.

Finally, it was time for the fighters to gather and go to the United Center. The UFC set up two different departure times for the fighters. The first departure time was for the undercard fights and the second time for the main event. Leaving for the arena was similar to the process we went through for the weigh-in the night before. Burt met us in the mat room. He gathered the fighters and the seconds into the room and gave his speech. His speech consisted of professionalism, showmanship, expectations, and responsibilities of the fighters and their camps. The room was completely silent during Burt's dialogue. As he spoke, I scanned the room. Tension and nervousness were visible on everyone's face. I'm sure my face was no different.

Shortly thereafter, we were guided downstairs to the buses. Once again fans were all around, wishing the fighters good luck and cheering, and like before it filled me with a unique sense of importance, a feeling that my purpose in Chicago mattered. We boarded with half of the fighters and their camps on one bus and the rest on the other. Then we hit the road towards the United Center.

The half-hour bus ride felt like a day long, cross-country trek. As we exited the bus and stepped into the back door of the building, the cameramen were already recording footage they could use during the production. Burt was directing everyone to their respective dressing rooms.

We were escorted to the Chicago Blackhawks dressing room where we shared a locker room with three other fighters. The dressing area had an attached room with a nurse and doctor who would be addressing any injuries that might occur throughout the night. In the center of the area were two 15'x10' mats. A representative of the Athletic Commission constantly monitored the room.

We unloaded our gear in the corner that was marked with a sign labeled "Roop" and began to situate ourselves. Burt then announced the fighters from our dressing room who were allowed to enter the Octagon. We marched into a stadium filled with loud music and empty seats. The place was enormous, but utterly vacant. I briefly thought about how exhilarating it would be to compete in front of so many fans. The biggest crowd I competed for was in the hundreds, their attention focused on several matches at one time, yet this stadium would be filled with over 20,000 fans, watching every move each fighter made.

This was my first time in an official UFC Octagon. The floor did not have as much spring as I was expecting, but was surprisingly soft. I trained in many different cages but I never felt canvas like this. The cage was filled with fighters and their cornermen. It was interesting how each fighter would do something different. Some joked and took pictures in the Octagon with their camps. Others rehearsed standing up against the cage. For others, the cage was nothing more than a backdrop to their conversations with other fighters.

George was not joking; we were there to fight. We began working on visualization exercises. George started in the blue corner and Ed in the red. I acted as the referee and we would run through the start of the fight over and over as if the other fighters weren't there. We practiced it just as we had done a month earlier in George's home gym.

Back in the dressing room, fighters began to warm up and stretch their muscles. As they worked Thai pads and focus mitts, camera crews captured close-up shots of each fighter to use for the television production of the night.

An official from the Athletic Commission brought in a pair of gloves with the UFC logo. To prevent any tampering with the gloves to make them harder, the UFC supplies each fighter with a brand new pair for every fight. New gloves are stiff and cumbersome and do not form well to the fighter's hands. To help fix this problem, Ed and I each took a glove to begin breaking it in. We rolled the glove from side to side and front to back, softening the padding to make it a better fit for George's hands.

While George got dressed, in walked "House." House's full name is Don House. He is one of the two most recognizable cutmen in the fight game. As a cutman, House was responsible for wrapping

George's hands prior to the fight and treating any cuts or swelling that could occur. George specifically requested House to be his cutman. They met on the set of *The Ultimate Fighter*. While on set, George broke his hand and House took care of him and his hand, allowing George to continue fighting on the show.

House was a personable man with a calm demeanor. While he wrapped George's hands, Ed and I continued breaking in the gloves. They were still stiff, but getting softer. House kept our minds occupied by sharing stories from how a knee injury kept him from being an alternate on the 1984 Olympic boxing team to the Mayweather vs. Pacquiao controversy to his experience as a cutman. When House finished wrapping George's hands, the Athletic Commission representative overseeing the process signed the wrapping and the tape around the bottom of George's gloves.

Next to enter the locker room was the referee, Big John McCarthy. John McCarthy is a famous mixed martial arts referee. During the growth of the sport, he was in charge of every major fight that took place, punctuating the moments before every round by asking the fighters, "Are you ready? You ready? Let's get it on! Come on!" That night, he was supervising George's fight. Big John asked George if he had questions about the rules, the fight, or the commands he would use. He followed up by saying, "I know you've been here plenty of times, but I just want to make sure."

"We rollin', we rollin'! This is what we do! All night long, baby!"

was heard coming from the hallway.

All week I was told how Burt roamed the halls yelling, keeping his tightly-run ship on course and not drifting a bit; this is exactly what he was doing.

"Roll to the hole!" Burt hollered.

One by one, fighters were called out of our locker room and to the cage, mirroring a scene in the movie *Gladiator*. Once a fighter left, we could hear the entrance music rumble throughout the stadium and the crowd's reaction to the action. The remaining fighters were half watching the fights on the closed circuit television in the locker room and half shadowboxing and shadow-wrestling to keep their bodies loose and their minds occupied.

"Roop!" Burt shouted from the hall.

George was up. We shot out of the locker room and strutted down the hall to the entrance arch. I imagine at this point George's heart rate was registering at about 130 beats per minute, because mine was at least 150. We stood at the entrance to the arena for two minutes, but it seemed like an hour. As we waited, I peered over my shoulder and saw Cub standing right behind us. I could see the nerves in his face as well.

The cameramen and producers stood in front of us, directing us where to stand. "Five, four, three…" Suddenly, the music commenced and we were headed out to the cage. Earlier we discussed the need to keep the fans from touching or disturbing George on the way out. There have been plenty of examples of fans exhibiting inappropriate actions towards fighters en route to the Octagon. I have seen fans grab a fighter's hat off his head while walking to the cage and another occasion when someone leaned over the fence and kissed BJ Penn on his way to the Octagon for a title fight. We wanted to assure that no one distracted George in any way. I was on George's right side and Pierre was on his left. We walked out between George and the crowd to make sure no one could touch him.

Immediately upon arriving to the cage, the referees and Athletic Commission checked George one last time and rubbed Vaseline on his face before he entered. The three of us circled around to our side of the Octagon and dropped the sponsor banner. Cub arrived and the door was shut. Bruce Buffer introduced the fighters. We circled to our cage-side seats while George and Cub stared at each other. The preparation was over. It was time.

CHAPTER 10: THE FIGHT

Are you ready? Are you ready? Let's get it on!" Big John shouted out. The fight was on. The first round was action-packed. Neither fighter was afraid to throw. George was doing an excellent job of keeping Cub at a distance. Cub was stalking while George kept him at bay with a jab and a front kick, catching Cub every time he advanced. At one point, Cub threw a spinning wheel kick and the crowd cheered.

Despite Cub missing the kick, George found himself backed against the fence in Cub's corner. He fought his way out of the corner and circled back to the center of the cage. Cub's frustration was evident and he began to come in straight forward, just like we predicted. The fight was going as planned. Then George attempted a takedown; Cub stopped the takedown and scored a hip toss. George scrambled to his feet and finished out the round.

George was bleeding from the nose after the first round. House headed into the Octagon with Ed as I circled around the outside of the cage. Ed was honest with George and told him he lost the round because of the takedown. Ed instructed George to maintain working the leg kicks, which were more effective than we intended.

He also reminded George to throw a knee as Cub began to advance and to throw the wild punches.

Clack! Clack! Clack!

The notification sounded alerting the seconds to leave the Octagon, so we returned to our spots and the second round was on its way. The fight began just as exciting as it had left off. George and Cub continued to throw flurries. George was caught by what looked to be a solid punch, but it didn't seem to faze him. The next exchange, George threw the knee Ed told him to use but it just grazed Cub's chin. Cub persisted to stalk George with his hands held low, like he had done on the tape. George threw a left hook at the same moment Cub threw an overhand right. Cub's strike landed flush, knocking the mouthpiece out of George's mouth and dropping George to the canvas. Cub swarmed onto George and rained strikes onto his prone form. Just like that, it was over.

Forty-five days of preparing, sweating, bleeding, planning, visualizing, and sacrificing had come to a dramatic end. My heart sank. Very few times in my life had I felt as helpless as I did at that moment. The doctors and referee attended to George, who was coming to realize what had just taken place, and there was nothing I could do about it. I stood still and watched my friend pick himself up and show as strong a face as he could. I had no idea what to do. The prospect of defeat had not even entered my mind when helping George for the fight, and yet here we were.

George stood next to the referee as Bruce Buffer announced the winner of the fight and Big John raised Cub's hand. George showed his sportsmanship by shaking Cub's hand and left the cage. On the way back to the locker room, the crowd showered George with compliments and words of encouragement. The crowd showed a man they had never met, talked to, or maybe even recognized a great amount of empathy in a way I hadn't expected.

We exited the arena and sat in the doctor's examining area, comprised of two chairs facing away from each other separated by a black curtain. The area was for both fighters. George sat on one side of the black curtain while Cub sat on the other side. The doctor examined George and then we went to the locker room.

None of us spoke much besides answering questions about the fight as George asked them. Intermittent words of encouragement and reassurance were expressed, but we didn't want to dwell too long on the situation. Each one of us was or had been an athlete at some point and knew it was best not to talk about it for some time.

Before long, a man arrived to tell George his check was ready and he was to report to a room down the hall. A short amount of time had passed since the fight and I wanted to ensure George wasn't feeling any adverse effects from the blows, so I accompanied him to the room to receive his check. George and I talked briefly about the fight and I could tell he was slightly embarrassed about what happened. I looked at George and said, "Dude, I just want you to know that I'm proud of you."

"I'm probably going to get cut," George said as we sat back down in the locker room. "That's fine though. I'll just pick up some fights and get back in."

"We'll see what happens. You fought hard, George Roop," Ed chimed in. "And if we have to go kick some guys' asses to get back here, then that's what we'll do."

The rest of the night was spent in the locker room watching the remaining matches with the other fighters and their corners. I had an excellent conversation with Greg Nelson from Minnesota Mixed Martial Arts Academy. Nelson had been the main trainer for Sean Sherk, former UFC Lightweight Champion, and Brock Lesnar, former UFC Heavyweight Champion. In the martial arts world, Nelson was a legend in his own right for his outstanding Muay Thai and by being a former collegiate wrestler. I wasn't going to let the chance slip by to possibly have some of his wisdom rub off on me.

Once the fights concluded, we loaded onto the bus. George came to grips that he was getting cut after being knocked out for the second time in the UFC. It wasn't just George who had a rough night though. Every fighter in our locker room was defeated. In fact, everyone who fought out of the blue corner lost that night.

We sat towards the front of the bus. Sitting directly in front of George and Ed were Joe Silva and Sean Shelby, the two matchmakers for the UFC. They are two powerful men in the UFC and also the same two guys who would be letting George go.

"So who are you thinking for your next fight?" Shelby asked George. George's face lit up. As George and Ed spoke with the matchmakers, the mood began to lighten in the Roop camp. Despite the loss and suffering a highlight-quality knockout, George's aggressive style of fighting had not gone unnoticed.

We were up at six the next morning to catch the plane back to Tucson. The trip was spent with most of the crew sleeping or playing video games; few words were uttered on the flight. Despite the loss, the mood was still very positive, and we were already discussing the next fight.

CHAPTER 11: DOWNTIME

The next year was chaotic. George and I both had a tremendously busy year full of life changing events. George and his fiancée had their second baby and welcomed a little girl to their family and married in April.

The night before George's wedding, Ed fought on a Bellator card in Atlantic City, New Jersey. Of course, George made the trip with him. Everyone involved in the wedding was apprehensive whether George and Ed would return in time for the wedding. But they knew each other well and depended on the other to be in their corner.

Unfortunately, Ed lost by decision to Marcos Galvao. There was no dominating moment during the fight for either fighter. Although I personally believed Ed was the better fighter, on that night, Ed had a tough time getting his momentum going and time slipped away. The following morning Ed and George were on the plane en route to Tucson.

For me, it was back to life as usual after returning from George's fight. I was exhausted from the mental, physical and emotional effort that was invested into the week. There was no time to rest though. The next day, I was to report to my new position at work at six in the morning. I was promoted to supervisor after eight years in law enforcement and was elated about the way 2012 was commencing. I had just been a part of a UFC event, promoted at work, began my new venture Fight Log Media and Bernice was moving to Tucson in March. My life was on track and heading in the right direction.

A week after getting back from Chicago, on February 7, 2012, I received a call that Delmar, my step-grandpa, passed away. Granted it was expected, the news hit me like a ton of bricks. Delmar unceasingly gave me his support and the encouragement to work hard. When I was in high school, I played on some of the worst teams. My varsity team had a total of one win in thirty-four games over the span of four years. Undeterred by my team's losses, he and Grandma attended every home football game. He would tell me the next morning over coffee, "Well at least you didn't get skunked." He saw the best in everything and everyone.

I will miss him dearly.

The month of March proved to be remarkably busy. Bernice relocated to Tucson, and I launched www.fightlogs.com. The subsequent months were exhausting and stressful. I was getting accustomed to living with a girlfriend, learning to balance my new position at work, teaching at Boxing Inc., running the company and training. It was physically and emotionally taxing but completely worth it.

As the old adage says, time really does pass quickly when you are having fun because 2012 came and went in a blur. I competed a few times in some smaller tournaments with mixed success. I won my division at a North American Grappling Association (NAGA) tournament only to get dominated at the Las Vegas Open the following August.

Defeat is never easy for me to swallow. However, the older I become, the less it seems to matter. I realized that had I submitted the whole bracket in Las Vegas, the result would likely be the same—I would return to Tucson and punch the clock at work as usual and with few exceptions, no one would know. When I first began competing, I entered every match with a narrow mind expecting to win every match. Back then, I felt like I could be like BJ Penn, who earned his black belt after three and half years, which is very uncommon. Now, eight years later, I look at competition through more mature eyes. I no longer view matches as a measure of my worth as a man, but rather a personal test to see whether my hard work on the mats would be rewarded. On that particular day in Vegas, the answer was no.

As for George, he had his difficulties throughout the year as well. He was forced to pull out of two fights. We were training for a fight scheduled for July against Antonio Carvalho when he aggravated a back injury that plagued him since the Hioki fight. Over that previous year, we were forced many times to stop practice because of a pain that would shoot down his back and into his leg, and as the frequency and intensity of the pain increased, it prevented him from training.

After the disappointing injury in July, George called me. "Hey man, I want to get your opinion on something. I think I'm going to see if the UFC will let me drop down to 135. What do you think?"

This wasn't the first time George broached the subject. He fought once at 135 against Eddie Wineland in January of 2010. The weight cut was grueling and the fight did not go well. Many people in our circle speculated the drop to 135 to be a bad idea. Be that as it may, George suggested dropping back down a couple times and this time he was serious.

I didn't know what to say. A fighter who was coming off back-to-back losses and knew his next fight was paramount to his career was asking me, a guy who has never had a professional fight, what he should do.

I replied, "Look, I think you should make the cut. Here is why. If you don't make the cut to 135, the entire time you are preparing for your next fight it will be in the back of your head that you should be down a weight class. You can't have something like that in the back of your head. You need to win your next fight and you have to have full confidence going into it."

Even though George is 6'1", he is not as heavy as most 145-pound fighters. Getting ready for the Swanson fight, George came close to the weigh-in weight a couple times. Most fighters at that weight are cutting from 170 to 180 pounds down to 145. George, on the other hand, was starting from 157-160. I believed the cut to 135 was achievable. Prior to the Wineland fight George was fighting at 155 pounds. Dropping two weight classes at once was harder on his body than this weight cut would be since George had been fighting at 145 for the last couple years.

Eventually, he determined his next fight would be at 135. The UFC matched him with Yuri Alcantara in January of 2013. George was scheduled to fly to Brazil and fight the rising Brazilian fighter. Unfortunately, shortly before the fight was scheduled, George suffered a bad cut during training that required multiple staples in his head, again forcing him to pull out of the fight.

CHAPTER 12: CHINA

When George was cut during training, I was exploring China. Bernice's father was working overseas and invited us to visit him in Shanghai over Christmas. I admit, for a small town mama's boy, China was not my first choice in places to spend my Christmas. Traditionally I try to go home to Nebraska for the holidays. But how could I refuse a once in a lifetime trip like this? Never having left the country before, I never dreamed I would travel to China.

When we first made the decision to make the trip, the first thing I did was find a gym. Since Shanghai was a city of 24 million people, I imagined there would be a place to train. Sure enough, Shanghai Brazilian Jiu Jitsu (SBJJ) was located within a mile of the apartment we would be staying at.

Bernice asked if I was really going to pack my gi and take it to China, reminding me that it was going to be extremely cold and I would need room for heavier clothes to wear during the day. For me, there was no way I was going to travel to the other side of the world and not get some training in. How many people in the U.S. can say they have trained in China?

I simply retorted, "If it gets that cold, I'll just wear my gi top around town."

She responded with a chuckle, shaking her head. I was pumped and anxious to see what the gym would be like.

The trip to China made me apprehensive. Considering my lack of travels outside of the United States I didn't know what to expect. I envisioned myself going to Europe or Australia, but China was a whole different ball game. The more I thought about it the more nervous I became. How will I know where I am going? How will I read the signs? Will I be capable of ordering food? How will I know what I'm eating?

Bernice's family spoke Cantonese, which originates from the Hong Kong and Canton areas of China, but the official language of Mainland China is Mandarin. Before meeting Bernice, I wasn't aware of the innumerous dialects in the Chinese language. Since the written language was the same for both, I imagined the disparities in Cantonese and Mandarin to be similar to British English versus American English; the languages vary slightly but you can still communicate. In reality the comparison is closer to French and Spanish which are markedly different.

Bernice's dad taught himself Mandarin and had no trouble communicating with people from Mainland China. However, he worked during the day and we were left to on our own during his absence. This left me even more concerned and to an extent I think it bothered Bernice as well.

After stepping foot in China, my fear quickly dissipated as nearly all the important signs were written in both English and Chinese. I was astonished at the number of Chinese people who spoke English as well. Nearly everywhere we ventured, we encountered someone who spoke either English or Cantonese making our travels more pleasant.

China itself was breathtaking. We were fortunate to take in some amazing sites including the Great Wall of China, the Forbidden City, and the Emperor's Summer Palace in Beijing and the Oriental Pearl Tower in Shanghai. The country was steeped in an unbelievable history and mystique.

I couldn't help but think of the constant contrast the whole country had. Cities brimmed with newly built modern skyscrapers amidst beautiful ancient buildings and landmarks that had survived thousands of years. Sidewalks were filled with commuters who didn't own cars. Many walked by foot or rode bicycles, while the streets were packed with brand-new BMW's and Porsches. An apparent large income gap existed between the general public and the upper class.

The weather was unbelievably cold, even for a boy from Nebraska. I was beginning to think Bernice was correct in saying I should have left my gi at home and packed more warm clothing. But after a few days in Shanghai, it was time to put the gi to use. I was overwhelmed with nerves and excitement. Before leaving for China I sent the gym an email asking if I could drop in for a class. Over a span of seven years, I visited a number of different schools with mixed reactions, including an incident when I was told I wasn't welcome to train. Fortunately, SBJJ was accommodating and welcomed me with open arms. They replied to my email stating they would love to have me in the class and provided me with their training times. Due to our busy itinerary, the only class I could attend was a Tuesday class at noon.

I was unaware of what to expect from visiting a school in China. I didn't even know what language the instructor spoke. To make matters a little worse, Bernice and I lost our way to the gym making us slightly late to class. In the United States, there is a running joke that schools run by Brazilians never start their class on time. Class times on their schedules are more an approximation, versus the American way of beginning promptly at the listed time. The common experience of waiting for your Brazilian instructor to show up is known as being on "Brazilian time." Luckily for me, this culture also bled into China. We arrived ten minutes late as other students were just showing up too.

The gym was located on the third floor of an office building. Sitting outside the entryway was a shelving unit with cubbyholes for students to place their shoes. I introduced myself to the instructor, who remembered me from the email I sent the week prior. The instructor's name was Stanley Tam, a brown belt who was originally from Hong Kong. I let out a sigh of relief as he greeted me in English and discovered nearly everyone in the class was an immigrant from Europe, Australia or Hong Kong, which made communicating much easier than expected.

The class structure was no different than it is in the States: a warm-up followed by drilling, then technique, and ending with open sparring. Since it was noon on a Tuesday, the class was smaller and consisted of a dozen students, mostly beginners. This didn't stop me from wanting to roll with all of them and I nearly did.

Toward the end of class, I had an opportunity to go against Mr. Tam. I learned an important lesson in 2008 right after I received my blue belt - never wrestle aggressively with the instructor. In 2008, I was training too hard with the instructor at a gym called the Lion's Den. The instructor, who I imagine was trying to calm me down or prove a point, fell back into a foot lock from my guard that had me tapping in a hurry. The pain was excruciating and my foot immediately turned black and blue. The instructor apologized, but I could tell I pushed my limits that day. I took the lesson in stride as I limped out of the gym after class.

Rolling with Mr. Tam was much different. He was very technical with great flexibility, making his guard challenging to pass. We took turns sweeping each other back and forth. From my peripheral vision I noticed that the rest of the class quit training and were watching us roll. We exchanged position after position with neither of us getting the better of the other. Suddenly, while I was attempting to sweep him on to his back, out of nowhere he snatched my arm, catching me in an arm bar.

The experience was fantastic! Jiu jitsu guys can sit and talk about the art for hours, regardless if they know each other or not. It was no different at SBJJ. After class Bernice and I stayed to chat with Mr. Tam about different styles and moves that were popular in China versus what was popular in the U.S. I was reluctant to leave, but our full itinerary forced my hand and we departed, sorry to have to end the conversation.

The remainder of our vacation in China was spent being tourists. We tasted different foods, even though ordering food merely meant pointing to a picture on a menu. We also toured museums and attended an acrobat show. After ten full days, it was time to say goodbye and fly back to the States. As wonderful as an experience China was, I was ready to be home.

CHAPTER 13: GETTING BACK ON TRACK

On the flight home, I was still under the impression I would be traveling to Brazil for George's fight with Alcantara. My phone was turned off and I didn't check any emails the entire time I was away. When we landed in Phoenix, George called and told me he had received a cut on his head during training. While sparring at his gym, George was taken down against the cage when his head struck a wire sticking out from the bottom padding of the cage. The wire caused a nasty gash, which required staples to close. He was forced to pull out of the fight. Luckily, the injury was not worse but that cancelled our trip to Brazil.

A few weeks later, George contacted me. A new fight was on the horizon. The UFC set him up to face Ruben Duran. At the time of the news, I knew nothing about Duran. George sent me fight footage of the bantamweight. Duran was a thick 135 and appeared to be incredibly strong. I was confident, barring getting caught with a hard shot in an exchange of strikes, that George was going to dominate the fight.

The match took place in Canada. Despite being invited to go, I was unable to make the trip. KJ was to be married in San Diego the same day and I was not going to miss my best friend's wedding. That didn't change my nerves, though. We put in numerous hours prepping for that fight and I was just as edgy as if I had been cage side.

The fights were streamed online so I packed my laptop for the journey to San Diego. The fight and the wedding were taking place nearly at the same time. Many people attending the wedding trained with George, so I wasn't the only one dying to watch the outcome. A half hour before the ceremony, many of the wedding guests, including the groom himself, were huddled around my laptop in the hotel bar, watching with nervous tension as George controlled the fight and won a unanimous decision. That was the start of a sensational night!

George concluded the fight with very little trauma. After a couple weeks off, he was back in the gym and lobbying for his next match-up. Finally, George texted me in early April.

"Got my next fight. Brian Bowles UFC 160."

Holy crap, this is a test. Brian Bowles was the former champion at 135 but had not fought since November of 2011. Bowles was dangerous. Watching his fights for years, I have always been a fan.

Bowles is a ripped 5'8" and equipped with heavy hands and a dangerous guillotine choke that latches on quick. We had our work cut out for us.

The timing of the fight worked out impeccably. UFC 160 took place on May 25th. Two of our main training partners also had matches coming up at the same time: Chris Cariaso was fighting at the UFC in Brazil event on May 18th, and Anthony Birchak was fighting for the Maximum Fighting Championship's (MFC) bantamweight title in Canada on May 11th. This was perfect; we would have a guy from our camp fighting every week for three straight weeks.

I was preparing for the USA Wrestling Grappling World Team Trials in April. FILA, the governing body of international wrestling, was trying to introduce other wrestling styles into the international system since 2007. Jiu jitsu was one of these styles, which they titled 'gi' and 'no-gi' grappling. I went to the trials in 2009, but I was out of my league. In 2012, the trials were cancelled but I was selected as an alternate through a petition process. This year I was thrilled about going.

Trials didn't go as I visualized. When I competed in 2009, I remember the tournament going smoothly without much controversy about the rules. This year the rules meeting reminded me of a sandlot football game when I was a kid where rules were created beforehand, or worse—after the game started. This was just the beginning.

My first match did not go as planned. Right off the bat I gave up a horrible takedown, but recovered and got the sweep. Shortly after there was a slight scramble where I was able to lock up a head and executed a tight arm choke. A head and arm choke normally involves pushing the opponent's shoulder into his neck, cutting off his carotid artery on one side of his neck and applying pressure to his other carotid with an arm. My opponent was resilient and tough as nails as he fought it off for over a minute. I couldn't believe it; I exhausted my arms by squeezing too hard. The rest of the match I was worthless making low percentage submission attempts. I lost by a score of 4-2. My first match was over and already my hopes of a spot on the no-gi world team were gone. Now in the losers' bracket, the best I could finish was third.

Following the competition, the referee who officiated my first match approached me. He apologized to me. Apparently when I applied the head and arm choke, I should have been awarded three points for moving to side control. The rules were hazy at best and varied greatly from most jiu jitsu competitions, so much so that not even the referees fully understood the point systems.

I continued on, winning my next match and then losing my third, but my competitive fire disappeared after I dropped my first match in an unimpressive and exhausting fashion. Regrettably, the gi division didn't go any better when I finished second out of a whopping two competitors. I lost to Jayson Patino, who had an impressive grappling history that included participating in the Mecca of all no-gi tournaments, the Abu Dhabi Combat Club (ADCC).

I was distressed over the defeats. Competing in any sort of fashion to represent my country had always been a dream of mine. Now that particular dream was over. A couple of weeks after the trials, FILA and USA Wrestling announced they would no longer hold any world games for grappling. Over the previous six years, participation and quality of competition fell significantly and they now ceased holding such events.

Back in Tucson, there was no rest for me as I dedicated myself to help the three fighters in their training camps. George sent me video footage on Bowles. I studied the fights repeatedly, combing the footage for weaknesses in Bowles' game.

I noticed many times when Bowles threw a jab he would duck his head to his right and slightly drop his right hand. This was ideal because one of George's best weapons was a head kick with his left leg. The more I watched, the stronger my gut feeling became: George was going to knock this guy out.

CHAPTER 14: THE WOLF PACK

The time for their competitions drew near. Anthony was on his last week of preparations and Chris was arranging to leave for Brazil to finish his last two weeks of training there. In the past month, the five of us had grown close, all supporting and pushing each other to our limits.

The week before Chris and Anthony left, a photo was taken of us inside the cage in Chris's gym. I added an excerpt from a Rudyard Kipling poem to the picture. The poem was the perfect embodiment of the training that had taken place. Giving a fighter the confidence that he prepared properly for his fight is important. The poem summed up our training camp nicely. I attached it to the picture and sent it to everyone.

Now this is the Law of the Jungle -- as old and as true as the sky;
And the Wolf that shall keep it may prosper, but the Wolf that shall break it must die.
As the creeper that girdles the tree-trunk the Law runneth forward and back
For the strength of the Pack is the Wolf, and the strength of the Wolf is the Pack.

-Rudyard Kipling-

From left to right: Anthony Birchak, Chris Cariaso, Jay Petersen, Jerome Gage, George Roop

If it served no other purpose, it was entertaining to everyone after the term "Wolfpack" had been made into a joke by the movie *The Hangover*. The crew took to the photo and "Wolfpack" quickly became the training camp's nickname.

After six hard weeks of training, the fighters were ready for their matches. I was working and was unable to watch the fight, but Anthony fought first and won a unanimous decision over a tough Ryan Benoit. Wolfpack's record was 1-0. Undoubtedly, Anthony was becoming one of the brightest future stars in MMA.

The next weekend was Chris's turn. Bernice and I huddled around my computer at a local Barnes and Noble to watch the fight.

Observing my friends fight never gets easier, especially when I have to keep my voice down in a public place like a bookstore. Chris started slow with his opponent, Jussier Formiga, getting the takedown and moving to mount. Chris repeatedly escaped as Formiga regained the dominant position. Despite losing the positional war, Chris avoided any damage. This continued through the first two rounds.

Eventually, in the third round Chris began fighting with a sense of urgency. He was cognizant he lost the first two rounds, and Chris wasn't going down quietly. He began the third round by picking up the pace. Chris put an exhausted Formiga on his back and landed heavy hands on the Brazilian. He exhibited big heart by putting such a beating on Formiga but sadly, it proved to be too little, too late. If you examined the two fighters after the fight, you would have thought Chris won, but because of the positional advantages imposed by Formiga early on, Chris lost by unanimous decision. Wolfpack dropped to 1-1.

I was crushed; Chris and I had only known each other for a year but became good friends. I saw the pressure he put on himself, and knew he didn't perform how he wanted to in the first two rounds. All I could tell him was, "You are a warrior."

CHAPTER 15: UFC 160

Now it was George's turn.

The next Thursday I met George, Ed, and Pierre in Las Vegas. George and Ed made the trip earlier in the week, but Pierre and I worked until Thursday.

Two weeks leading up to the fight, George had an independent film crew, *El Reporte MMA*, follow him to his training sessions. Never one to love attention or being on camera, it was nerve-racking for me. I did my best to avoid the camera and limit interviews, but the publicity was good for George, so I did what I could to be cordial for his sake.

Once I arrived at the MGM Grand, where we were residing and the location of the fights, I could tell the attitude was different than the Chicago fight. Unaware if it was because of the more drastic weight cut, the pressure of the fight, or if there was an elephant in the room that I just couldn't see, the mood was far from the relaxed atmosphere that existed in Chicago. It seemed everyone was on edge and out-of-sorts.

In town for only forty-five minutes, we were already on our way to the mat room to get the last training session in. George was behind on his weight cut and he needed to burn as many calories as possible before the weigh-ins. As we turned the corner to go to the mat room George sprinted and ran down the stairs located between two escalators. As George jogged to the mat room, I glanced over to see Brian Bowles standing on the other escalator staring at George. Tension was thick.

Our training session that night did not go well. George's transitions from position to position were not as smooth as normal. While wrestling on the mats, it felt like we were an old couple attempting to dance with our shoelaces tied together. Everything George did seemed to be filled with tension, which killed the fluidity of his movements. Ordinarily I would have been worried. Yet some of my most recent readings and seminars I attended dealt with Dr. Jared Porter's ideas that there is a need for "contextual interference" in training. Dr. Porter theorizes that poor practices right before a game leads to better performance at game time. Exhibiting a lack of routine or added distraction (contextual interference) is beneficial to stimulate better performance. Therefore I took the training session with a grain of salt. The important thing was to get a good sweat and cut the weight, not fret over the fluidity of George's ground game.

George's weight cut was much more strenuous this time compared to the Duran fight. Although he hit 135 at weigh-ins, it took a toll on his body. After cheating so many times on his diet before the fight, he paid the price when it came time to make weight. Not being strict with his regimen was uncharacteristic of George. I believe accepting the Bowles fight so soon after his fight with Duran played a role in the diet mishaps. Cutting that much weight requires your diet to be scrupulous, but being so strict for sixteen weeks versus just eight weeks, the discipline is harder to maintain. Following some refreshing liquids and proper meals, George was back up to 156 by bedtime.

Time flew from my arrival on Thursday night to Saturday. I felt like I just arrived yet it was game time. The morning of the fight was spent at the craps table in the MGM. On one hand, I didn't want George to be around all the smoke from the casino, but on the other he also needed to keep his mind occupied. Dealing with a little secondhand smoke seemed a much better option than sitting in the hotel room overthinking the fight.

Hours passed by like minutes. We shared a semi-private locker room with Donald "Cowboy" Cerrone, one of the UFC's more colorful personalities. I found small irony in the fact that when we were in Chicago fighting against Cub, his corner man was Greg Jackson, and this time we were sharing a locker room with Cowboy, whose corner man was also Greg Jackson.

George's fight was one of the first fights on the card. Once again we were in the blue corner locker room. Prior to the Swanson fight, I never noticed the blue corner mostly meant the underdog corner. The fighters exit their rooms to the cage at separate times. The underdog fighter comes out first and is assigned to the blue corner, and the favorite enters second and is assigned to the red corner. Everyone, except the people training with George, felt George was the underdog, so it was back to blue corner again.

"Roop! You're up, baby!" Burt screamed from the hallway. We grabbed our bucket of ice and towels and followed Burt toward the walkway. No one said a word.

We waited impatiently at the entry to the arena. The crowd was loud and surprisingly fuller than I anticipated for an early fight. Next to us at the entryway stood a monitor projecting the live feed being played on the broadcast. They briefly displayed a snippet into Bowles' locker room. Bowles was practicing blocking head kicks from the left leg, the same strike I predicted George would win the fight with.

"He's going to be looking for that head kick," George said.

I nodded in agreement.

Right as the music began to play, I leaned over to George and advised, "Just keep your left hand high and everything will be fine." I knew the surefire way for Bowles to win would stem from the hard punches of his right hand, similar to the punch that stopped George in his fight against Cub. George nodded and we were on our way to the cage.

George entered the Octagon cage, followed quickly by Bowles. Bruce Buffer, the UFC ring announcer, introduced the fighters and the cage was locked. As Buffer's signature line goes, "It's time!"

The fight started off strong for George. He landed strikes from a distance without getting involved in heavy exchanges. George established a jab to keep Bowles on the outside. As Bowles moved in to exchange, George kept his left hand high and used his footwork instead of exchanging punches like he had done with Swanson.

The fight was going George's way. Bowles looked up at the clock only halfway through the first round. This is normally a sign the fighter is getting weary. I was feeling terrific about the round, then...SMACK! George was caught by a hard right hand that dropped him to the canvas. The punch occurred in almost the exact same area in the cage where Swanson knocked George out.

George was struggling to get to his feet when he got locked into a tight guillotine. My heart was sinking, but I knew if anyone could escape the guillotine choke from Bowles, it was George. I just spent eight weeks trying to choke him with that exact same choke with very little success. Suddenly, George rolled to his back still stuck in the guillotine. He was now facing us and it looked tight.

Ed yelled, "Don't worry, George, you can sit there all day. Only forty seconds left!" *Forty seconds? That's a long time!* I thought to myself. Suddenly, Bowles released the choke. Perhaps Ed's words helped encourage the release. I was ecstatic. George fought off the same choke that Bowles used to submit some admirable opponents.

The horn sounded and the round was over. Ed and I moved into George's corner. I placed ice on his chest and back while Ed talked.

"Did he steal that round?" inquired George.

I determined Bowles won the round because of the hard shots and the guillotine attempt. Though, in my eyes George had been winning the round for the first four minutes.

"No! You won that round," Ed answered, keeping George's confidence up. Ed talked him through the strategy for the next round, reminding him to utilize the range and kicks to the body. George nodded in agreement.

One of the commission officials yelled, "Seconds out!" instructing Ed and me to leave the cage. We hustled out and round two commenced.

Settling back into our cage-side spots, I peeked over at Bowles. He was already out of gas. His muscular frame seemed swollen from lactic acid and he was breathing from the mouth. The look on his face intimated that he would rather be doing anything at that second other than fighting.

Round two began the same as round one. George employed his range and landed solid jabs and a kick to the body that appeared to take all the fight right out of Bowles. Roughly a minute passed and Bowles had not thrown a punch, which Ed announced to everyone within earshot. "He hasn't done anything in forty-five seconds George! Forty-five seconds!"

Then, Bowles lunged in to throw a punch. Just as we scouted, he ducked his head to his right and stepped forward with a jab. George countered with an unyielding jab of his own, knocking Bowles to the ground. George quickly moved in to capitalize on the opportunity, landing heavy strikes to Bowles on the ground. Bowles reached to grab George's leg in hopes of pulling up with a single leg, but he was unsuccessful and ended up on his hands and knees.

George continued to throw hard punches, and finally a hard shot collided with Bowles' face that dropped his head to the mat. He was clearly hurt, and the referee, Herb Dean, stepped in and stopped the fight.

George just defeated the former bantamweight champion of the world and one of the most dangerous fighters in the weight class by knockout. Very few people outside the blue corner saw this coming.

Ed, Pierre and I were shouting and yelling as Ed climbed on top of the Octagon. George ran to Ed, pulled him into the cage and pretended to strike Ed. It was easily one the most unusual celebrations that had taken place in the UFC. However, it was all pre-planned. Ed had done the same thing in his recent knockout in Bellator.

"I told you, Roop!" I shouted. Deep in my heart I knew he was going to win by knockout after watching the fight footage, and George proved my hunch right.

It was the biggest win in George's career.

The ability to endure the lows and accept the highs is a common ingredient of success. With his win over Bowles, George put together his first two-fight win streak in nearly five years. His journey, though far from over, has not been easy. Since this fight I have often thought about our time in Chicago. The disappointment of losing to Swanson in such a dramatic fashion would have been enough to break many people. Compound that loss with the series of injuries George endured the rest of the year could have made the 31-year-old contemplate a new career. The bad matchups, injuries and devastating losses would have been enough to break the focus of many fighters.

Our journey initiated with George asking me to help him prepare for a fight, but it wasn't George who got the most out of our relationship. If I have helped him win, that effort is dwarfed by the lesson he taught me by exposing me to the attitude necessary for success. George's story is a useful lesson for many of us. We have the blessing of going through our own personal struggles or losing streaks. It's our reaction to the mishaps that defines our character. We can take the simple way and change our direction, or we can keep moving forward.